Praise for *Fully Awake and Truly Alive* and Rev. Jane Vennard's Work

"A wise, helpful and nourishing book, filled with personal stories and practical guidance."

—**Marcus J. Borg**, author, *Meeting Jesus Again for the First Time*

"Jane Vennard presents a spiritual path for practical feet, a guide for finding the seeds of prayer, reflection and nourishment in a delightfully spacious way. [This is] is a blessing for all of us who, as our lives go faster, yearn for divine healing and companionship in the still, small voices of the soul."

—**Wayne Muller**, author, *Sabbath: Restoring the Sacred Rhythm of Rest*

"Jane Vennard has given us guidance that is both simple and profound, practical yet very mature, personal yet social. Her wisdom about prayer is what we need."

—**Richard Rohr**, O.F.M Center for Action and Contemplation

"One of the most extraordinarily helpful books I have ever read on the relationship of our deep bodily-emotional selves to our spiritual unfolding. Combines practicality with personal sharing, wit, poignancy and deep spiritual insightful wisdom."

—**Flora Wuellner**, author, *Prayer and Our Bodies*

"Ilumines a broad spectrum of spiritual practices, making them available and accessible to all who seek to enrich their lives. [Invites us] on a journey inward toward the home that awaits us within and on a journey outward in meaningful connection to those around us."

—**Victor Kazanjian**, dean of Intercultural Education & Religious and Spiritual Life, Wellesley College

"We wake up through Jane Vennard's words to recognize the innate spiritual nature of living immediately and directly into our experience of our bodies, into silence and solitude, into community, hospitality and service…. Our response is gratitude for Jane Vennard's masterful teaching."

—**Dwight H. Judy, PhD**, professor emeritus of spiritual formation, Garrett-Evangelical Theological Seminary; author, *A Quiet Pentecost: Inviting the Spirit into Congregational Life*

"Vennard's concise introductions to spiritual practices and forms of prayer will enrich the prayer lives of both individuals and groups. This book will help readers become open and available to the grace and generosity of the Holy Spirit."

—**Joseph D. Driskell**, Pacific School of Religion

"The work of a master teacher, and like all master teachers, Jane Vennard is clearly in love with her subject. She is in love with the honest, spirit-stretching questions people have about prayer. She is in love with the stunning multitude of ways people can engage in spiritual practice. Drawing deeply from her personal experienced, she leads her readers into the joy—and humility—of helping others discover the life-filling richness of prayer."

—**Steve Doughty**, pastor; author, *To Walk in Integrity*

"On a personal level, I was unexpectedly rewarded to have my own spiritual life challenged and enriched by my encounter with Jane Vennard's mind, heart and spirit in this volume."

—**Howard Clinebell, PhD**, author, *Anchoring Your Well-Being*

FULLY AWAKE

AND

TRULY ALIVE

SPIRITUAL PRACTICES TO NURTURE YOUR SOUL

REV. JANE E. VENNARD

Foreword by Rami Shapiro

Walking Together, Finding the Way®

SKYLIGHT PATHS® PUBLISHING
Woodstock, Vermont

Fully Awake and Truly Alive:
Spiritual Practices to Nurture Your Soul

2013 Quality Paperback Edition, First Printing
© 2013 by Jane E. Vennard
Foreword © 2013 by Rami Shapiro

For information regarding permission to reprint material from this book, please mail or fax your request in writing to SkyLight Paths Publishing, Permissions Department, at the address / fax number listed below, or e-mail your request to permissions@skylightpaths.com.

Library of Congress Cataloging-in-Publication Data

Vennard, Jane E. (Jane Elizabeth), 1940–

Fully awake and truly alive : spiritual practices to nurture your soul / Rev. Jane E. Vennard ; foreword by Rami Shapiro.

pages cm

Includes bibliographical references and index.

ISBN 978-1-59473-473-1 (quality pbk.)

1. Spiritual life. I. Title.

BL624.V46 2013

204'.4—dc23

2012045514

10 9 8 7 6 5 4 3 2 1

Manufactured in the United States of America
Cover Design: Jenny Buono
Interior Design: Heather Pelham

SkyLight Paths Publishing is creating a place where people of different spiritual traditions come together for challenge and inspiration, a place where we can help each other understand the mystery that lies at the heart of our existence.

SkyLight Paths sees both believers and seekers as a community that increasingly transcends traditional boundaries of religion and denomination—people wanting to learn from each other, *walking together, finding the way.*

SkyLight Paths, "Walking Together, Finding the Way" and colophon are trademarks of LongHill Partners, Inc., registered in the U.S. Patent and Trademark Office.

Walking Together, Finding the Way®
Published by SkyLight Paths Publishing
A Division of LongHill Partners, Inc.
Sunset Farm Offices, Route 4, P.O. Box 237
Woodstock, VT 05091
Tel: (802) 457-4000   Fax: (802) 457-4004
www.skylightpaths.com

For
Margaret Johnson
and
in memory of
Sister Louise Hageman, OP

We entreat you, make us truly alive.

Fourth-century prayer of Serapion of Thmuis

CONTENTS

2. THE PRACTICE OF REST

3. THE PRACTICE OF SILENCE

4. THE PRACTICE OF SOLITUDE

5. THE PRACTICE OF LETTING GO

Releasing Your Attachments, Your Past, and Your Future

6. THE PRACTICE OF COMMUNITY

Discovering Support, Encouragement, and Interdependence

7. THE PRACTICE OF HOSPITALITY

Inviting, Welcoming, and Nurturing the Stranger

8. THE PRACTICE OF SERVICE

Cultivating Generosity, Kindness, and Joy

9. THE FRUITS OF PRACTICE

Living Gratefully, Humbly, and Compassionately

FOREWORD

What I'm about to say may trouble you. In fact, I hope it does.

Here you are reading the foreword to *Fully Awake and Truly Alive* and you are most likely half asleep; maybe even more than half. You've probably grown so accustomed to sleep living (a far more common experience than sleepwalking) that you mistake your current state for wakefulness. Well, it isn't. You are asleep, and so is almost everyone you know. And on the off chance you do know someone who is awake, she probably seems so strange to you that you avoid her as best you can.

Of course being asleep doesn't mean you aren't functioning. You get up and go about meeting the obligations of your day. You may eat well, exercise regularly, and cultivate loving relationships. You may, if asked, confidently (if a bit humbly) admit to being happy and not a little successful. It isn't that you're lying, it's that being asleep you have no idea what kind of happiness awaits you when you wake up. So you are a little fish swimming back and forth in a tank, completely unaware of the vast sea that is your true home.

Chances are, though, you have moments when the tank seems too small—instances where you sense something greater, when you sense *you* are something greater. These are moments when wakefulness trembles at the edge of consciousness, but you label these moments as unreal and dismiss them so that you might go back to the truly unreal you call reality.

If any of this is true, if you prefer sleep to wakefulness, the unreal to the real, you shouldn't read this book.

Jane Vennard, the author of *Fully Awake and Truly Alive*, wants to wake you up. Or, more accurately, she wants you to wake yourself up by engaging with the spiritual practices she shares in this book. If you'd rather stay asleep, give this book to a friend. But if you are curious about waking up, let's be clear as to what you are waking.

In the Bible Moses tells us, "See I have set before you this day life and death, blessing and curse. Choose life if you would live" (Deuteronomy 30:19). To choose life is to wake up, and when you wake up, you wake up to the entirety of life: living and dying, blessing and cursing. You can't escape any of it, but you can learn to navigate all of it with equanimity and even joy.

As long as you remain asleep, you imagine that there is a way to live without death and curses, without the suffering you ascribe to bad luck or karma or punishment of some kind, or that there is a test that, if passed, takes you out of this world into a heavenly utopia. And as long as you entertain this fiction, you will look for a way out, a way to escape. But when you wake up, you realize there is no escape and no need to escape. You wake up to each moment as an opportunity to serve others, to bring a little light into the gray world in which most of us live.

When you wake up, nothing changes and everything changes. Nothing changes in that there is still living and dying, blessing and cursing, hope and horror. Everything changes in that you no longer resist any of it. As Ecclesiastes teaches: when it is time to cry, cry; when it time to laugh, laugh; when it time to birth, birth; when it is time to die, die (3:1–8). The world keeps spinning one moment to the next, but you no longer try to stop the spinning, for you have learned to twirl right along with it. This is the promise of wakefulness: not a new world, but a new you.

Reverend Vennard is fearlessly awake to the wild dance of life. Rather than sleeping through life, she awakens to it. Rather than escaping from reality, she embraces it. Rather than distracting herself with a life to come, she dares to live the life that is. And she wants you to do all this as well.

Read this book. Live this book. Wake up.

—Rami Shapiro

INTRODUCTION

Spiritual practices could be called life practices ... because they
help us practice ... aliveness, alertness, wakefulness, and humanity.

Brian D. McLaren

For the past twenty-five years I have been teaching about prayer and
spiritual practices in seminaries, churches, and retreat centers. When I
began, I thought my task was to give participants an overview of common
practices from my Christian tradition. I shared the history and
methods of Centering Prayer, *lectio divina* (sacred reading), fasting, worship,
and service. I also introduced some practices that were not as well
known, such as walking the labyrinth and chanting the music of Taizé.
In addition to my lectures, we spent time doing these practices together.

Many people found these presentations interesting, but the information
didn't translate into a regular pattern in their lives. They
might begin to read the Bible a little more reflectively after a lesson
on *lectio divina*, some might practice the method of Centering Prayer
when it was convenient, or they might walk a labyrinth if they happened
across one. But nothing fundamental seemed to change. As this
realization slowly dawned, I began to question what I was doing. I
wondered if there might be other ways to teach about prayer and spiritual
practices that would not just change a few behaviors, but could,
possibly transform lives.

Expanding Our Understanding of Prayer and Spiritual Practice

To help people explore their own understanding and experiences of prayer and spiritual practices, I started opening my classes and workshops by asking people to write down ten prayer methods or spiritual practices they regularly engaged in. I discovered that most participants were unable to come up with more than five. If I changed the language of the question and asked them to write down the many ways they nurtured their souls, refreshed their spirits, or honored the holy in their lives, many were able to get to twenty. Along with activities traditionally thought of as spiritual practices, they would mention such things as making music, watching the sunset, gardening, talking with a friend, baking bread, reading poetry, taking long bike rides, playing with grandchildren, or chopping wood.

As the lists grew, I invited participants to consider whether the activities they were naming might be thought of and experienced as prayer or spiritual practice. This suggestion was usually met with stunned silence. Playing with a dog a spiritual practice? A long run around the park a form of prayer? However, as they began to consider this possibility, the discussion grew lively, for they had to reconsider what they believed about spiritual practice and what they had been taught about prayer. I was asking them to remove prayer and spiritual practice from whatever box they had stashed them in and take a new long look at the larger possibilities. As people continued to share experiences and opinions, someone would inevitably ask, "What is the difference between prayer and spiritual practice? Are you using these terms interchangeably? Are they really the same?"

Defining Terms

I was taught in my Christian tradition that there are many spiritual disciplines or practices and that prayer is one of them. Within the category of prayer are many different types of prayer, such as praise, petition, confession, and intercession. Each type of prayer can be expressed in a variety of ways, such as using words, moving, being silent, or making images. The tradition offers rich possibilities in its teachings about prayer, but I felt that the placement of prayer as one form among many other spiritual practices was artificial. What if the traditional practices such as worship, fasting, or service in the world were actually forms of prayer? What if all those activities that nurture our souls and refresh our spirits could be experienced as either prayer, or as spiritual practice, or both? What would happen to our definitions and categories?

Giving up the traditional categories freed me to expand my old definition of prayer to include all spiritual practices. I was also able to explore the idea that all spiritual practices could be experienced as prayer. In addition, this way of understanding freed me from the common language of prayer, which many people feel necessitates a belief in a personal God.

As I shared these ideas through teaching and writing, I received much affirmation. People resonated with this expanded definition of prayer, and the possibility that prayer and spiritual practice could be synonymous. But not everyone! The objections came from a variety of places. Some traditionalists were unwilling to stretch their understanding of prayer beyond the boundaries of what they had been taught. They thought these new definitions were confusing, and they preferred the old categories. Another objection came from people within religious traditions who were questioning the relevance and efficacy of prayer. Their images of God had been shifting away from a personal God who was the "other," who could be praised and asked for things, who could offer comfort and forgiveness. They imagined a God who was, as described by Christian theologian Marcus Borg, "in all and beyond all"; by theologian-activist Dietrich Bonhoeffer, "the beyond in our midst"; or by Christian philosopher Paul Tillich, "the ground of being." They wanted to engage in spiritual practices that would draw them toward and into the holy Presence, but they were no longer comfortable with old concepts of prayer.

Others who objected to considering prayer and spiritual practice as synonymous were Buddhists, whose tradition is not theistic. Many Buddhists do not consider their practices to be prayer. For example, a

Buddhist friend once said to me when she was experiencing a struggle in her life, "Please, don't pray for me." Yet later, when I was ill, she told me she would "hold me in her meditation." She needed to separate prayer from her practice of meditation.

In addition, atheists and secular humanists, who have no belief in a god, do not pray, but many of them engage in spiritual practices. I realized that if I were to reach those outside the Christian tradition, as well as those within the tradition whose images of God and old beliefs were breaking down, I needed to carefully examine the ways I write and speak about prayer and spiritual practice.

In this book I have sought to find language that will include believers, non-believers, and those whose beliefs are in flux. As one of the latter, I still claim my Christian identity, although I no longer hold tightly to many of the traditional beliefs. I have come to think of myself as a *practicing* Christian rather than a *believing* Christian. This renaming has liberated me from the struggle of agonizing over what I believe and has allowed me to turn my attention and my energy to the practices of other traditions as well as my own. This variety of spiritual practices has helped me understand and experience what I believe to be the core teaching of Christianity—what it means to be human and truly alive.

Becoming Fully Alive

On a recent trip to Australia I was invited to co-lead an ecumenical retreat. The committee sponsoring the event suggested we call the workshop "Becoming Fully Alive—Spiritual Practice as a Way of Life." I discovered they were drawing on the wisdom of Saint Irenaeus, a bishop and doctor of the Church in Lyons, France, who wrote in the second century, "The glory of God is the human person fully alive." Irenaeus's words echoed across the centuries and supported my new ways of thinking about prayer and spiritual practices. They provided a working definition that I hope will resonate with you: spiritual practices are those ways of seeing and being in the world that help us wake up and become fully, truly alive.

My intention is that this understanding and way of defining spiritual practices can include those of you who go to church, synagogue, or temple and those who do not; those of you who are comfortable with God talk and those who aren't. For traditional believers, this definition does not leave God out and can affirm traditional forms of prayer and practice. For those whose image of God is shifting and changing, the possibility of becoming fully alive can be congruent with a nonpersonal God. If you have no belief in God, maybe becoming fully alive, not for the glory of God, but for the sake of living an awake and authentic life, resonates with you. Becoming fully alive challenges all of us to find among the infinite number of spiritual practices the ones that are right for us.

Examining Our Practices

When we examine lifelong practices, we may realize what we have been doing for years is still viable. "What I love about retirement," a longtime pastor said, "is that I don't have to preach the sermons I prepare." When he realized that preparing for weekly sermons had been an important spiritual practice during his active ministry, he decided to continue the discipline in his retirement. Studying the biblical text, reading commentaries, looking for present-day applications of the passages helped him be fully alive. "I missed that weekly practice when I retired," he explained. "So now I do the preparation but am relieved of the stress of preaching. It may sound odd, but I delight in this practice."

On the other hand, a retired clergywoman confessed that she no longer attended church. As a pastor, leading morning liturgy had been a regular activity. She was nourished by the rituals as she guided others into worship. However, she often longed for the day she could sit in the pew with her family, with no responsibility. But now, only a few months into her retirement, she had no desire to be in church on Sunday morning. "I've dropped out of worship," she said. "Church no longer feeds my soul. I leave feeling empty and sad. I would much rather be at work in my garden."

Both these people had the courage to examine their engagement with traditional practices and discern for themselves the degree to which these practices helped them be fully alive. Those of you who do not have traditional practices to examine can look to your regular daily or weekly activities and ask the same questions. Does your daily walk feed your soul? Do family dinners refresh your spirit? What about following world news? Volunteer activities? Reading poetry? Sometimes we fall into patterns of behavior and never stop to examine them to see if they are truly beneficial. We can all ask ourselves, "Is what I am doing helping me to wake up to being fully aware and present to life as it is? What activities deaden and diminish me and, therefore, what might I let go of? What new practices might I consider that could open up my seeing and being, and lead me toward wholeness and healing?"

As you consider possible practices, keep in mind that practices may be structured times set aside for such activities as meditation, study, service, writing, or exercise. Practices may also be what we do spontaneously as we remember to pay attention and respond to what is happening in life around us and within us. Such informal practices might include simply noticing when you are hungry, not filling open time with technology, letting go of a fixed opinion, seeing the beauty in a stranger on the street, recognizing your anger and deciding whether or not to express it. In the Buddhist tradition, these two kinds of practices—structured/formal and spontaneous/informal—are often categorized as *on-cushion practices* and *off-cushion practices*.

On Cushion, Off Cushion

For students of Buddhism, on-cushion practice is formal meditation time set aside regularly for the solitary or communal practice of mindfulness. Different methods of meditation may be used, but this discipline of time apart is at the center of Buddhist practice. However, the real purpose of meditation practice is to take what is learned on cushion into everyday life. Buddhists see every moment off cushion as an opportunity to practice mindfulness.

A teaching story is told about the man who meditated diligently, spending years in solitary practice in a mountain cave. He finally broke through all that was holding him back and became enlightened. He arose from his cushion, left his cave, and strolled blissfully down the mountain. When he reached the marketplace he found himself surrounded by busy, rushing people. When a woman accidently stepped on his foot, he struck her. On-cushion practices by themselves do not necessarily integrate the fruits of practice into daily life.

For spiritual practices to guide our awakening, we need time and attention on cushion and off cushion. Although we usually think of formal on-cushion practices leading to informal off-cushion practices, I believe this movement is not linear, but circular. The structured periods of formal practice lead us to informally practice awareness in our daily lives, and the spontaneous moments of practice can guide us back into formal intentional practice. Because many of the people I work with have tried and failed many times to establish a formal practice, I find it useful to introduce off-cushion practices as a way to encourage becoming fully alive.

This starting place does not ignore or deny the power of longer, planned periods of practice. Rather, it offers the opportunity to circle back to those times from a lived experience. For example, the person who begins to practice brief periods of silence in the middle of a busy life is more likely to schedule a day apart or even a weekend silent retreat than the person who has had no experience of silence. The person who is able to recognize the benefit of short naps may begin to move toward the possibility of regular Sabbath rest. This circular movement from momentary informal practices to more intentional formal practices, and around again to spontaneous practice, is possible in the spiritual practices I will be introducing.

A Variety of Practices

The practices I have chosen to explore in this book are: care of the body, rest, silence, solitude, letting go, practice in community, hospitality, service, and the fruits of practice—gratefulness, humility, and compassion. I do not believe that these are more important than other spiritual practices we could have explored. I selected them because I believe most of the world's religions recognize these practices in some form or other. Therefore, I will be able to draw on the wisdom of many traditions, providing a variety of lenses through which to view these practices. Since these practices are also encouraged in the secular world, and are often recommended by therapists and other health professionals, I will share from their resources as well. I hope to use language that is welcoming to all.

Each chapter includes explanations of the practice, illustrative stories, and invitations to practice in the moment. These off-cushion practices can be done in the midst of your daily life. Each chapter ends with the question "How are you called to practice?" designed as a review of the material and an opportunity to search your heart and mind to decide what practices are right for you. In addition, two or three step-by-step on-cushion practices will be offered for those of you who wish to spend more time with a particular practice and may desire additional guidance.

As you begin your exploration of the following practices, I suggest that you read this book in the order of your interest rather than necessarily beginning with chapter 1. Out of necessity, the chapters are numbered 1–9, but that linear order need not be followed. I tend to write in a fairly circular fashion. One practice folds back to a previously mentioned one, and you may find echoes of different practices throughout the chapters. Therefore, if the practice of hospitality calls to you, begin there. If you realize you are having trouble with the practice of letting go and want to explore this practice further, start with chapter 5. A friend recently told me she was having trouble with a nonfiction book many had recommended to her. "I got bogged down in the beginning and couldn't get clear enough to move on," she told me. I wondered aloud if she might skip around in the book, rather than trying to make herself read it from beginning to end. "Look for the chapters and topics of interest," I said. "Choose your own order, focus on the sections of interest, and skip what does not apply. You don't have to read the whole thing."

Just because we are alive and functioning does not mean we are awake! We all know how easy it is to sleepwalk through life. My hope for you as you roam through this material is that you find useful, immediate practices to wake you up to the wonders of life. We don't practice to make perfect; we practice to make possible. We don't practice to get somewhere; we practice to know we are already there. May the practices you discover, choose, and engage in serve as ways to continue your journey of being and becoming more fully alive.

1

THE
PRACTICE
OF CARING
FOR YOUR BODY

Finding New Images, Deep Wisdom, and Blessings

The practice of wearing skin is so obvious that almost no one engages it as a spiritual practice.

Barbara Brown Taylor

Spiritual practice begins with the body and depends on the body. In stillness or in motion, we are in our bodies. Alone or together, we are in our bodies. Silent, speaking, or singing, we are in our bodies. On some very deep level we know that our spiritual lives are fully integrated with our bodies, but we are likely to forget that truth. Children know that the body and spirit are inseparable. When I ask people to remember early childhood experiences of God, or holy moments in their young lives, their stories are always fully embodied. "Climbing trees was awesome to me," one woman told a prayer group. "I would sit perched high in the branches and watch people below. I believed I was seeing the world as God sees it."

"My fondest memories of childhood were those times when my large extended family would sing together," another participant shared. "As a little child I didn't know the words of the songs, but I would be caught up in the rhythms and harmonies, feeling safe and embraced by the voices. Those were holy times!" This instinctive knowledge of the integration of body and soul is often forgotten and left behind as we grow older. We may have been taught to *think* about God rather than to *experience* God. We may have been told that our spiritual lives transcend our physical lives, that the sacred is different from the ordinary, or that true holiness means we must deny our bodies. But I have discovered that, when invited, the reality of the integration of body and soul comes forward once again in people of all ages and traditions.

One of my favorite questions to ask participants in spiritual formation classes and on retreats is, "What nurtures your soul? What renews your spirit? When do you experience the Holy?" There are hundreds of responses, all embodied, just like the childhood memories. A Buddhist student recently reported that one of his spiritual practices is "walking with cows." He wanders in a cow field near his house, simply being with those large beasts, listening to the sounds of them breathing, eating, and moving.

"What renews my spirit is not physical activity, so maybe my spiritual practice is not embodied like so many others," an elderly man once shared. "I like to sit in a comfortable chair on my front porch when the weather is fine and simply watch the world go by." "Oh, you are embodied all right," someone challenged him. "You are sitting; you are looking. You can't do that without a body!"

INVITATION TO PRACTICE

Think of an activity that renews your spirit. How does your body participate in that practice?

Body Image:
Experiencing Your Body as a Gift

I once asked a new friend (who later became my husband) if he liked his body. He looked at me puzzled and replied, "Well, it's the only one I've got." His response, irrefutable and based in reality, brought me up short. I had spent so many years and so much energy being unhappy with the way I looked, wondering how I might improve, and wishing I were different than I was. I had tried to like my body, but had rarely succeeded. Jim's words shifted the issue from body image to a lived experience of my body.

I started to experience my body as gift. Unique. One of a kind. No other body like mine in the world. How wonderful is that! I began to focus on all my body had done for me over the years. It had taken me from place to place, hauled wood, baked bread, ridden bicycles, and danced in the moonlight. My body had grown and matured, had fallen ill and recovered, had been wounded and had healed. I had learned to speak and to listen, and to live with my mistakes; I had cried tears of sadness and of joy, and had been consumed by fits of giggles. I had loved, been loved, and made love. My body made my life possible.

INVITATION TO PRACTICE
Name five things your body is doing for you right now.

With this new awareness, I worked hard to let go of old distorted images of my body. It wasn't easy. I had been well trained. I grew up with a very narrow idea of female beauty. Slender, but not thin. Athletic, but not too strong. Tall, graceful, and restrained. Never big or loud or boisterous. Not only did I apply these criteria to my own body, I viewed other bodies through these same critical lenses. I had learned to judge bodies, not to admire them. All that changed one evening when I ventured into a communal nude bath.

I was visiting the Esalen Institute on the Big Sur coast of California. I was there for a workshop entitled "Women's Liberation from Within." I had no idea that part of the event would be to join the women of the workshop, as well as other women in the community, for song and conversation in the large hot tubs perched on the cliff above the ocean. I was terrified. How would I look to others? What would they think of me? I believed I would be sorely judged.

Slowly I emerged from the dressing room with a towel wrapped around me and my eyes lowered. I crept toward the edge of the nearest tub, dropped my towel, and slid under the water. Feeling somewhat protected and hidden, I raised my head and looked around. To my amazement women were casually sitting on the edge of the tubs or walking around to cool off. They looked so comfortable in their skin. No one seemed to be judging anyone. The women were tall and short, fat and thin, young and old and in between. There were children, one woman on crutches, and another with mastectomy scars. I sat with my mouth agape. Everyone was beautiful!

AN INVITATION TO PRACTICE
The next time you are with others, friends or strangers, let
your judgment drop away and notice the beauty in everyone.

This experience of looking with new eyes at the beauty of the human body, as well as the reminder that my body is unique and precious and the only one I've got, did not erase my old training. Although I do believe the words in the Hebrew scriptures (Genesis 1:26–27) that we are made in the image and likeness of God, I still look critically at my own body and can be quick to judge other bodies. But now I catch myself. I notice when I am being critical, and rather than judging, I gaze with wonder and curiosity at the incredible variety of human embodiment. The awe I feel leads me to love and honor my body and other bodies, and I am able to believe the ancient Hasidic wisdom: "Every time we walk down the street, we are preceded by hosts of angels sing-ing, 'Make way, make way, make way for the image of God.'"

Befriending Your Body

When we change our body image from dissatisfaction and disrespect to one of love and appreciation, we can begin to treat our bodies as our friends. To maintain and deepen friendships, we listen to our friends, are there for them in times of both need and celebration, give them tokens of our love and faithfulness, and stand by them over time and through changes of circumstances.

Forty years ago, when my friend down the street called to tell me her brother had committed suicide, I dropped everything to be with her. Years later, Jim and I flew across the country to be at her son's Bar Mitzvah. She always calls on my birthday; I send chocolate on Valentine's Day. When I was in deep despair, she listened to me tell my story over and over again. One day she gently interrupted me and offered a new perspective on my drama. She did not give me advice; she simply told me how she saw my struggle. Her words were like a splash of cold water as I awoke to new possibilities.

Our relationship has not been without bumps, but we have rid-den them together, coming out more committed on the other side. I moved away from the old neighborhood twenty-five years ago. With distance separating us, and with both of us aging, we are finding new ways to maintain this long and beautiful friendship.

Reflecting on this example of deep friendship, consider the ways you give to and receive from your friends, and imagine how you might treat your body in a similar fashion. Do you listen to your body, allowing it to tell you when you are hungry, need exercise, or desire rest? Do you celebrate your good health, newfound strength, the appearance of a few gray hairs, or a newly acquired skill? What about giving it small tokens of appreciation, such as a new haircut, a soak in a hot tub, or a lie-down in the middle of the day? Are you able to stay faithful to your body when illness strikes, when accidents hap-pen, or when your energy is not what it was when you were younger?

AN INVITATION TO PRACTICE
Take a moment to listen to your body. What is it telling
you? How is it asking you to pay attention?

Treating our bodies as we treat our best friends may not be our usual pattern. We are more likely to ignore our bodies or treat them like beasts of burden that carry us from place to place. We grudgingly take care of them, but with no appreciation or joy. Sometimes we simply take our bodies for granted. If we are unhappy with our bodies, we attempt to fix them or "whip them into shape." When our bodies cause us trouble, we may get angry with them. We complain about what they are doing, such as feeling sick or gaining or losing weight. We whine about how our sprained ankle is keeping us from dance class or the ski slopes. We rage about the serious diagnosis and begin to feel that our body has betrayed us.

The sense of body betrayal emerged in each interview I conducted with people with chronic illness for my book *Praying with Body and Soul*. Although the tales were different in many ways, all of them reported that before the onset of illness their bodies were simply behaving as expected, as they always had. The diagnosis of AIDS or MS, a miscarriage, or the need for back surgery brought the sense that their bodies had betrayed them, leading them to feelings of disbelief, sadness, depression, and rage. Those interviewed reported their experiences with their bodies as similar to the times friends had betrayed them.

The friend who betrays us often becomes the enemy. So it is with our bodies. After an accident, during illness, and when aging, the spiritual challenge is to continue to cherish our bodies and not turn them into enemies. We need to become even better friends to our bodies—listening more closely, following their guidance, celebrating even the smallest signs of healing, and remaining steadfast and faithful even when nothing seems to be improving.

Although the people I interviewed used the image of enemy in their experiences of illness, the idea of the body as enemy and betrayer makes no sense in Buddhism. In that tradition, experiences of physical suffering are understood to be a natural and necessary part of life and are not to be labeled pejoratively, for doing so would keep us from accepting things just as they are. Understanding the body's true nature, which is one of constant change and decay, inspires us to see the interconnection of all of life.

We often promise to stand by our friends and loved ones no matter what happens. This commitment to another is deepened by practicing the small rites and rituals of friendship. So it is with our bodies. When we practice honoring and caring for our bodies while they are healthy, practice tending them lovingly when little things go wrong, we increase the likelihood that we will have the wisdom and the skill to befriend our bodies in times of crisis. When our bodies receive this love and respect, they gift us with wisdom of their own.

Embodied Wisdom

If I were to cross my arms, put a frown on my face and shout, "I'm *not* angry," I imagine you would believe my body rather than my words. We know that our bodies reflect our thoughts and our true emotions. What we may not realize is that the body can guide our minds and feelings as well. If I am facing a difficult meeting in which I would like to be open and receptive as well as strong, I can put my body in a position that reflects my desired attitude. Sitting tall with my feet on the floor and my hands softly open in my lap or on the table, I will begin to think and feel more receptive. Our bodies participate in our spiritual practices in the same ways, both reflecting and guiding our spirits.

Catholic priest and spiritual teacher Henri J. M. Nouwen wrote in his book, *With Open Hands*, that if we approach God with hands clenched into fists, we will not be available to God's grace. If we approach with open hands, however, we make ourselves ready to receive God's blessings.

INVITATION TO PRACTICE
Make your hands into fists. Feel the tension up
through your arms. Offer a prayer of gratefulness
from this position. What is that like? Now open your
hands. Feel any change in your breath. Offer a prayer
of gratefulness from this position. Can you feel a
difference in your prayers?

Sometimes our body's wisdom will surprise us. I enjoy teaching people simple movements to the Lord's Prayer. Many tell me that with their bodies involved they experience that familiar prayer as if it were brand-new. In another activity, I invite retreat participants to put their bodies in four different prayer positions: hands folded and heads bowed, hands open in laps with eyes open, arms raised and heads tilted upward, and reaching out for the hand of another. Participants are amazed to discover the different prayers that come with each position. "I cannot express awe and thanksgiving with my head bowed," one woman exclaimed. "I need to have my eyes and my heart wide open." "When I clasped hands with another," a teenager said, "I found myself praying first for the person on my right, then the one on my left. Soon my prayer expanded to include the whole community." The sense of touch moved this young man's practice out into the world.

Connection to others is at the heart of the Buddhist tradition's teaching of loving-kindness. This practice calls us to be mindful of how we touch people, animals, and all things. As we touch the world gently, we are more able to express love and compassion for everyone and everything around us. It is as if our spirits are in our hands.

Our bodies do not only guide our spirits. They are also instruments in expressing our prayers, our longings, our awakened spirits. The connection between body and spirit can be seen in Muslim daily prayer. Jon M. Sweeney, author and spiritual teacher, writes in *Praying with Our Hands*, "The Prayer has several stages and universes of meaning: standing, bowing, prostrating, and kneeling all use the hands to recognize and praise Allah ('God' in Arabic) in humility and devotion."[1]

In the Sufi tradition, dancing or "turning" allows the body to become the doorway through which the Divine and human meet. As the dancer, or dervish, spins in circles, he or she holds the right hand facing upward toward heaven, and the left facing downward, returning the energy received from the Divine to the earth.

As we recognize the connection between heaven and earth, between body and spirit, we can practice engaging our senses to remind us to pay attention to that reality. A friend of mine once began a list of things she saw, heard, touched, smelled, or tasted that reminded her of the presence of God in the midst of her life—birds in flight, the laughter of children, cold water on a hot day, baking bread, puppy fur, rainbows, the gentle touch of a friend, incense, singing, the signs of early spring—the list went on and on. Other phrases that could begin a list might be: "I wake up when I see ..., hear ..., touch ..., taste ..., smell ..."; "I become fully alive when I ..."; or "I am grateful when I...."

—◡◡◡—

INVITATION TO PRACTICE

Choose your opening phrase, and then simply open your senses to what is around you in this moment. Do not wait until you go somewhere else. Do this here and now.

I have come to call these lists *sensual prayers* or *sensual practices*. With our knowledge and experience of the transcendent rooted in our senses, we are able to stay connected with the Holy at all times. Whether alone or in community, in nature or an urban setting, in a mosque, temple, or church, our senses are ready to sniff out the

Divine. Remember feeling the warm sun on your back or the shock of plunging into a cold lake. Have you ever let rich, dark chocolate melt on your tongue? What of the sight and sound of Canadian geese taking off to fly north in their perfect V? Or the smells of an outdoor market selling local produce? Or the sound of an organ sweeping through a cathedral? Surely these are sensual experiences that may also have tinges of the erotic.

Sexuality and spirituality have long been disconnected in many of our cultures. One is low, the other high. One is bad, the other good. One is to be denied, the other pursued. After beginning to explore the possibility of healing these cultural dualities in a class in seminary, I overheard a student during break exclaiming into her cell phone, "I can't believe it! We're talking about sex in prayer class!" I am not sure if she was delighted or appalled, but whichever, we were bridging the divide.

As sexual creatures we can be guided into union, not only with another but also with All. The ecstasy of our bodies can teach us about surrender, bring us into the present moment, and remind us of another way we can be fully alive. Jan Phillips, author of *Divining the Body: Reclaim the Holiness of Your Physical Self*, invites us to "climb back into our bodies and remember the feel of sexual energy racing through our beings from head to toe. Remember the bliss of union, the sounds of delight, the tears and trembling in the face of oneness."[2] Our bodies have the wisdom and the means to heal the long-experienced separation between body and soul.

Healing the Divide

Both the Jewish and Christian traditions unite body and soul; however, the view of that integration is slightly different. In Jewish thought, the human is seen first as a body. The body is then breathed into and enlivened by the spirit. This understanding makes human life impossible without the integration of body and spirit. In Christian thought, however, humans are seen first as spirit. The spirit is then housed in the body. This difference may seem inconsequential, but I believe it has led the Christian church into a gross misunderstanding of the goodness of both body and spirit.

Saint Paul wrote in his letter to the church in Corinth, "Do you not know that your body is the temple of the Holy Spirit?" (1 Corinthians 6:19). This would seem to affirm both body and spirit, but over the centuries people began to change the imagery, and instead of the spirit being held in a temple, they began to imagine it housed in a cage or a prison. That shift led to the belief that the body needed to be broken and the spirit set free. Although the violent punishing practices of medieval times have largely ended, the denigrating view of the body continues within many parts of the Christian tradition. Returning to Paul's original words in scripture will help us view the body as necessary and sacred to human life. The body will reclaim its rightful place in spiritual life and practice.

In the Buddhist tradition, the understanding of the embodiment of practice is already present. Sogyal Rinpoche, author of *The Tibetan Book of Living and Dying*, teaches his students that the awareness of the body is to extend from formal meditation practices into daily life activities, such as handing a cup of tea to another person or working on your knees in the garden.

Exploring the role of the body in spiritual practices may help us discover that "in spite of differences in the doctrines and practices of world religions, embodied prayer plays a central role in all of them," as Jon M. Sweeney writes in *Praying with Our Hands*. "The unity in diversity is explicit in the somatic expressions of faith."[3] I believe that the separation of body and spirit, the degradation of one and the elevation of the other, can be healed. The healing begins with each of us as we practice caring for our bodies, valuing our embodiment, and opening ourselves to the wisdom deep within.

How Are You Called to Practice?

You have been gifted with the body you have. How do you plan to treat it, to care for it, to honor it as an integral part of your spiritual practice? I hope after reading this chapter you have more body awareness—paying attention to all the things your body does for you and the ways it helps you be truly alive. It might be wise to express gratefulness to your body every time you are aware of its many gifts.

Have old body images that were formed by messages from your culture, your religious tradition, or your family kept you from recognizing your unique beauty and treating your body as a friend? Take some time to examine these distorted images and let them go, replacing them with new images that reflect the truth of your embodiment. Barbara Brown Taylor, Episcopal priest and author, recommends we pray naked in front of a full-length mirror. She advises that it is "vitally important for your spiritual health to drop your clothes, look in the mirror, and say, 'Here I am. This is the body-like-no-other that my life has shaped. I live here. This is my soul's address.'"[4]

As you move through the world, notice when you open your senses wide and when you close down. My tendency is to allow my senses to wake me up to life when I am in beautiful places. However, I shut down in crowded urban settings, when I hear conflict and discord around me, or when I arrive at a place I feel is not safe. There is much to be experienced in the not-so-hospitable world—sights, sounds, smells that have the potential of waking us up to new realities, new possibilities, and a wider range of experiences that can help us become more fully alive.

If the celebration of the integration of body and spirit goes against the messages of your faith tradition, your family, or your community, you may find these ideas and practices foreign and intimidating. Try not to dismiss them out of hand. Instead, see if you are willing to consider them, testing them against your lived experience. Go slowly. Take your time. Treat yourself gently. There is no rush. The body is patient—it can wait a little longer.

GUIDELINES FOR MORE EXTENDED PRACTICE

WRITING A LETTER TO YOUR BODY

When I suggested to a group on retreat that they write a love letter to their bodies, one of the participants called out, "I'm not sure I can write a love letter, but I think I can manage a thank-you note!" If you are willing to try one or the other, begin by finding a quiet place, with paper and pen nearby or your computer open to a blank page.

- Settle yourself with a few deep breaths, let go of your plans for what you want to say, and open your mind and your heart to your wisdom deep within.

- Taking all the time you need, wait until the words begin to arise from deep within you. Consider the way you will address the letter, and then write the opening lines.

- If you let your feelings flow, you may be surprised to discover that the first paragraph or pages are neither a love letter nor a thank-you note, but rather a list of complaints and accusations. Do not censor your words; just keep writing.

- You may find at some point that your body wishes to respond to you, and your original letter becomes a dialogue. If this happens, see if you are willing to listen to what it has to say.

- Continue to write until there is a natural ending. Remember that in all good friendships communication is important and may need to continue.

- Do you want to promise to write again?

- When the writing is finished, sit quietly a few more minutes, paying attention to how you feel about what you learned, and the practices you may be considering to strengthen this friendship with your body.

BODY BLESSING

Blessing is a way we infuse the ordinary with holiness. In this body blessing we honor the sacredness of our embodiment. When offering blessings, allow the words to simply arise. You may find that no words are necessary as you offer a silent blessing to your body. Allow the blessings to unfold. When you are finished, remember that you can bless your body any time or place in the midst of your life.

- Find a place where you can sit comfortably and be undisturbed. You may wish to light a candle to mark this sacred time and place.

- Begin by attending to your breathing. Simply notice the breath flowing naturally in and out. Bless your breath.

- Turn your attention to your heartbeat. You may want to find your pulse or put your hand over your heart. Feel the steadiness of this life force. Bless your heart.

- Begin to focus on your feet—not just thinking about them but experiencing them. Feel your toes. Feel the pressure of your feet on the floor. Remember all your feet have done for you. Bless your feet.

- Look closely at your hands. Notice how they have aged. Make fists, open your hands palm up, turn them over. Press them together, rest them in your lap. Think of all the people your hands have touched, all the things your hands have made. Remember that your hands are used for giving and receiving. Bless your hands.

- Continue this rhythm of noticing, remembering, and blessing with other parts of your body—your back, your shoulders, your stomach, your genitals, your eyes, your ears. Take all the time you need.

- When the blessing is complete, sit quietly, attending to what it is like to feel so fully blessed. When you are ready, blow out the candle, and arise to go into the world as a blessing to others.

2

THE
PRACTICE
OF REST

Restoring Your Energy, Your Creativity, and Your Spirit

If we forget to rest we will work too hard and forget our more tender mercies.

Wayne Muller

When I was a child, my family spent two weeks every summer hiking in the mountains of Northern California. It was a glorious time. My father was relaxed, and the mountains renewed his spirit. As he and my mother walked along, I loved running ahead of them to see around the next bend and then returning to report. I would go off the trail to explore interesting trees and flowers and to climb on rocks. Sometimes I hid in the bushes so I could jump out to frighten my sister. I wore myself out in my enthusiasm and would periodically collapse in exhaustion.

All this time my father would hike steadily on, keeping the same pace going up or down hill or on level paths through meadows. His breathing was easy. His senses were open to the sights, sounds, and smells surrounding him. He would often comment softly to my mother, who walked a few steps behind him. He was a man at peace.

One morning when I had worn myself out running back and forth and around, I fell in a heap, declaring I was too tired to continue. He looked at me gently and said, "Jane, you need to learn to rest as you walk." I remember staring up at him in confusion. What could he mean "rest as you walk"? My nine-year-old mind could not comprehend the possibility. I thought my father must be teasing. I knew for sure you either walked or you rested. You couldn't do both at once.

When I told my spiritual director this story more than fifty years later she exclaimed, "Your father was a Protestant mystic!" I laughed her comment aside, saying, "Oh, no! My father was an engineer!" Then I realized I was again thinking with a dualistic perception of the world, just as I had as a child. At that time I couldn't conceive of resting while I walked, and now I couldn't imagine that my father had been both a mystic and an engineer. It was time to believe the wisdom of his early words, and in doing so, embrace the fullness of my father's life.

INVITATION TO PRACTICE
The next time you go for a walk, see if you can feel in
your body what it might mean to rest as you walk.

Cultural Perceptions of Resting

When exploring the spiritual practice of rest in a workshop or retreat, I ask participants what messages they have received from their cultures, their families, or their religions about resting. They are lively in their responses, relating a wide number of experiences. The most common response is that rest is only for the very young, the very sick, and the very old. Some people will share pejorative terms they have heard about people who rest during the day: "couch potato," "lazy bum," "slug-a-bed," or "good for nothing." Others may quote proverbs such as "Idle hands are the devil's playgrounds."

Only occasionally will I hear someone say that resting was not only accepted at home, it was valued. "My mother rested every afternoon from three to four, like clockwork. We learned to respect her practice," one woman shared. "But I am afraid I do not follow her example. I think I am just too busy to rest."

INVITATION TO PRACTICE
What messages did you receive about resting
from your family or religious tradition?

Twentieth-century Trappist monk Thomas Merton addressed this issue of over-commitment and busyness in a letter to a young friend. He advised him to discern what was most important to do and to let the other tasks go. "To allow oneself to be carried away by a multitude of conflicting concerns," he wrote, "to surrender to too many demands, to commit oneself to too many projects … is to succumb to violence."[1] When rest is not an integral part of our activity in the world, we are at risk of our actions becoming harmful to others and to ourselves. Our busyness and fatigue can cloud our judgment, and we are liable to say or do things we regret.

Another common theme I have discovered is that many people believe they do not deserve to rest unless they are exhausted—until they fall in a heap as I did by the side of the mountain trail. A woman told me of a time when she had gotten quite sick the month before she was to go on a long-planned trip. She was forced to cancel many appointments and attend to rest and physical therapy for her healing. When her departure date arrived, she was well and rested. "I felt guilty," she said. "I was leaving on a vacation that I didn't think I deserved."

The idea that we might rest before we are worn out, before we go on vacation, often strikes people as ridiculous. I worked with a busy pastor of a large church who was planning his sabbatical. He had decided to take his three months away from the church in the summer, when things at his congregation slowed down. "I'll really be tired," he said. "I'll have finished with the busyness of Easter; I'll have done all the planning for fall. I will really be ready to go." As I listened to him, I realized that he would leave on sabbatical exhausted. I wondered aloud if he might think of taking his sabbatical in the fall, giving him the summer to rest. He looked at me incredulously. Rest before sabbatical? Whatever for?

As we talked, he realized that the sabbatical he had planned would surely be a welcome change of pace and place, but it would be a busy time. He would be traveling, studying, writing—not resting. As we talked further, he saw the wisdom in planning his sabbatical for fall. The idea of leaving town rested, with everything in order, delighted him. He presented the idea to the leaders of the congregation, and although he had to do a lot of explaining and convincing, they finally agreed. When September arrived, he was able to leave the church with a clear mind and a light heart.

A light heart is not the attitude some people bring to resting. Instead, they experience resting as a chore. They see the need for rest as a sign of failure or weakness. They might say, "I was so tired I just couldn't keep going. I had to go upstairs and lie down." "I don't know what's the matter with me these days. I have to rest almost every afternoon." I, too, have experienced resting as a chore, but that was not what prevented me from experiencing the joy of an afternoon nap during a very busy and stressful time in my life. I was afraid that if I stopped my activities to rest, I might never get started again. I had images of myself going up to bed on an afternoon and staying there for days, maybe weeks. I imagined my life falling apart, slipping into indolence, never to be heard from again.

The spiritual practice of rest counters these cultural attitudes and celebrates resting as a natural rhythm of life. When we experience rest as a spiritual practice, rather than grumbling about the need for rest, we could exclaim, "Wow! What a great day. I was able to rest for three full hours!"

INVITATION TO PRACTICE
Notice your attitude toward resting.
What might it be like to rest before exhaustion?
How could you begin to celebrate resting?

This celebration of rest is expressed in a humorous exchange by the Australian author Michael Leunig in his book *The Curly Pyjama Letters*. In this story, Mr. Curly is a wise, optimistic fellow who, through letters, corresponds with his friend Vasco Pyjama, who has set out on a voyage of discovery. Vasco writes his mentor with a big question, seeking his advice:

> "Curly, I ask you as I ask myself each morning, 'What is worth doing and what is worth having?' These are big questions and I am curious about your answers. Yours cheerfully and entirely seriously, Vasco Pyjama."
>
> "Dear Vasco, I would like to say simply this. 'It is worth doing nothing and having a rest.' In spite of all the difficulty it may cause, you must rest, Vasco—otherwise you will become RESTLESS!"[2]

Restful Activities

Resting does not always entail lying down and taking a nap. There are other ways to rest. I remember my mother, who had been a mathematics teacher, balancing her checkbook when she couldn't sleep. "I find the numbers so relaxing," she would say. "They quiet me down." This may not be your idea of a restful activity, but she was wise enough to know what was best for her.

Some people find rest in the practice of Centering Prayer. Although this prayer form has its origins in the fourteenth-century Christian spiritual classic *The Cloud of Unknowing*, people of many traditions practice it today. Centering Prayer is an invitation to rest in God. In this form of prayer, we simply accept this holy invitation and sit in silence, with the intention of remaining in the presence of God for a set period of time. When we notice our minds have taken us away from the Presence, we invoke a prayer word to remind us of our intention. We use that prayer word only as often as we notice our attention has strayed. Teachers and practitioners of Centering Prayer will tell you that rest is at the center of this very simple, but not easy, form of prayer.[3]

Sitting quietly was not what a friend of mine needed after her husband had been quite ill, in and out of the hospital, into rehab, back home, and needing much care. He knew the toll his illness was taking on her, and as he began to heal and become more independent, he kept encouraging her to rest. "She just won't stop," he complained to me. "Now that I am better, she is going out and about, involved in projects and activities. I wish she'd rest." He didn't realize that what she was doing was restful for her. Being with friends, getting out of the house, and completing tasks brought rest to her soul after all the chaos and isolation of illness.

We need to be respectful of other people's needs for rest and ways of resting. As a colleague of mine has said about his marriage, "My wife finds working in the garden restful. I prefer to simply rest in my chair, enjoying the fruits of her labor!"

The practice of rest invites us to pay attention to our energy, notice our fatigue before it turns to exhaustion, and distinguish between different ways to rest. Sometimes I know that I am sleep deprived and simply need to go to bed earlier for a while. Other times I am weary; I might even call it "bone weary." Those are the times that the constant busyness has worn me down even though I have had good sleep and some afternoon naps. For me, that kind of weariness calls for a change of pace, which may mean more time to read, longer walks, or a leisurely lunch with a friend. The shift of rhythm is restful and restores my equilibrium.

INVITATION TO PRACTICE
What are restful activities for you? Plan to engage in at
least one restful activity this week.

Biblical Call to Rest

In the book of Genesis in the Hebrew scriptures, we read:

> And on the seventh day God finished the work that God had
> done, and God rested on the seventh day from all the work that
> God had done.
>
> (2:2)

In the book of Exodus, another word is added to the creation story:

> In six days God made heaven and earth, and on the seventh day
> God rested and was refreshed.
>
> (31:17)

In Hebrew, the word usually translated "refreshed" literally means
"and God exhaled." As I read those words, I feel the rhythm in my
body—breathe in, breathe out, breathe in, breathe out. We cannot
inhale if we do not exhale; we cannot create unless we rest.

INVITATION TO PRACTICE
Stop for a moment and simply notice your breath—inhaling,
exhaling. Feel the comfort of the rhythm in your body.

Paying attention to the creative energy in nature, we see the same inhaling-exhaling rhythm at work. The warmth of summer gives way to the abundance of fall. After the harvest, the winter land lies fallow, restoring itself for spring. Day cycles into night, and the moon grows full and then ebbs into darkness. We are surrounded by creation's rhythms of growth, productivity, and rest. If we attend to our own creative energy, we can find echoes of these natural rhythms.

I remember experiencing this creative rhythm in my own life when I was making the transition from teaching elementary school children to teaching adults. I spent hours reviewing the content of my upcoming continuing education class for teachers on creative classroom management. I tried to imagine standing in front of big people rather than little people. I made outline after outline, filling pages with lecture notes. Through a great deal of effort everything was in place, but I knew something was missing.

About a week before my scheduled presentation I went to bed in despair. I was sure I would fail at this new endeavor. I had a restless night but must have slept enough to let go of my struggle, for when I awoke I had the answer to what was missing: I needed to teach the adults the way I had taught the children. This did not mean I would use ten-year-old language; it meant that I would involve the adults in an experience of different forms of classroom management. Since I never lectured fifth graders for hours at a time, why did I think that adults would learn by sitting still and listening? If I were to teach teachers about creative ways to teach children, I needed to involve them in the process.

All the work I had done before that insight was useful; I simply needed to shape the material into a new pattern. It was a busy week as I transformed my notes into experiential learning plans. I invented interesting activities to involve my learners and designed a flow chart to assist the adults in moving from one activity to another. When the day came, I was ready. I was excited and filled with energy. It was surely not a perfect teaching/learning experience. There was some resistance from the learners, sometimes my instructions were confusing, and I had planned way too much for the time we had. However, I knew that experiential learning for adults was right and true. I had a lot to learn, but I was happily on a new path in my teaching career. Without resting and letting go of my anxious striving, there would have been no room for the new plan to arise to consciousness.

INVITATION TO PRACTICE

Remember a creative experience in your life when you discovered how resting or stepping away from the hard work led to an innovative solution.

Four Steps of the Creative Process

As you remember your own creative experience, consider whether your pattern is similar to these four steps of the creative process. First is the stage of *preparation,* when we work hard gathering information, analyzing data, reflecting on experience, and interviewing others. Then comes the *incubation* stage, during which we need to rest, to take a break, to attend to other things. We need to let go of trying to figure everything out, think everything through to completion. The image I use for this incubation stage is a game of pick-up sticks, when we toss the sticks into the air and see what pattern is formed in their landing. Up goes all that preparation so that a new idea can be born, one we most likely could not have come to with our rational minds.

The incubation stage may last a few hours, a night, or even many weeks or months before *illumination.* There is no guarantee the light will ever arrive, but without letting go and resting, we are likely to simply rehash old ideas, focus on what is already before us, rearrange the known facts, and never come up with anything new.

Finally comes the stage of *implementation.* Illumination is not enough. We must bring our insights and new ideas into the world, whether in the form of a work of art, an original solution to a management problem, or a new way of behaving in an old situation. In this way, our creative energy has the possibility of making a difference in our world.

INVITATION TO PRACTICE
Is there a problem or project in your life that would
benefit from a time of incubation? Would you be willing
to step away and enter a time of rest?

We have been exploring the biblical call to rest as part of the rhythm of nature and of the creative process. The emphasis has been on becoming rested, more energized, more useful. Rest has been in the service of our work in the world—resting to become creative and productive. Finding our own rhythm of work and rest is useful, and learning how to rest as we walk will serve us well. However, biblical scholars will tell us that if we stop there, we will have missed the full meaning of the tradition of Sabbath.

Sabbath Rest

In Jewish thought, the seventh day was not God's day off after the hard work of the first six. It was not an interlude between weeks of work. It was not a day of rest to prepare God for the tasks ahead. Rather, the Sabbath was a holy day, a day honored for the sake of life.

Looking at the Genesis passage carefully, we see that "God finished the work that God had done" *and* "God rested from all the work that God had done" (2:2). God both finished the holy work of creation and God rested. We usually think that the work was finished on the sixth day and the seventh was devoted to rest. But that is not what scripture says. We are told there was more to be done. What was God doing on that seventh day before God rested? "The ancient rabbis teach that on the seventh day, God created *menuha*—tranquility, serenity, peace, and repose—rest in the deepest possible sense of fertile, healing stillness," writes best-selling author and therapist Wayne Muller. "Until the Sabbath, creation was unfinished."[4]

When I first read this interpretation of the creation story, my mind was confused, but I felt a sense of wonder deep in my being. I realized that the prescribed day of rest is not only to restore and energize me for the work ahead; it is a day unto itself. Its only purpose is to let go of doing and having and striving in order to discover the gift of simply being. In the words of Jewish scholar Susannah Heschel, "Shabbat renews the soul and we rediscover who we are."[5]

Her father, Jewish scholar and mystic Abraham Joshua Heschel, author of the spiritual classic *The Sabbath*, understands the Sabbath, the seventh day, to be a sanctuary of time. Whereas the other six days are devoted to the tools of space, the building of civilization, this honoring of time creates not just a day but an atmosphere. Within this sanctuary of time we are able to practice those ways of being that are often ignored or forgotten in the world of space—pleasure, thanksgiving, restfulness, and delight. He writes:

> We must conquer space in order to sanctify time. All week long we are called upon to sanctify life through employing things of space. On the Sabbath it is given us to share in the holiness that is in the heart of time.... The clean, silent rest of the Sabbath leads us to a realm of endless peace, or to the beginning of an awareness of what eternity means. There are few ideas in the world of thought which contain so much spiritual power as the idea of the Sabbath.[6]

As Rabbi Heschel describes what the seventh day is to contain, he also offers us guidelines for what not to do on the Sabbath: "We abstain primarily from any activity that aims at remaking or reshaping the things of space." In other words, he tells us not to engage in "any acts that were necessary for the construction of the Sanctuary in the desert." Rather we are to be engaged in building the sanctuary of time. He even adds that on the Sabbath we are to refrain from all toil and strain, "even from the strain in the service of God."[7]

As you reflect on Rabbi Heschel's wisdom drawn from ancient scripture, you are probably wondering what his ideas might mean for your own practice of rest today. What might it be like to spend a day with no thought of work, to rest in the experience of being, to begin to explore what eternity might mean? In our modern day we long for help in doing that, but Rabbi Heschel does not offer us definitive ways to build and experience the sanctuary of time he so eloquently describes. We are not told how to practice Sabbath rest and accept the deep stillness that is offered. Without rules or guidelines, we are left on our own to simply accept the reality of the gift that is offered. In time we may know for ourselves *menuha*, that which God created for the world on the seventh day.

INVITATION TO PRACTICE
Choose one word or phrase from Rabbi Heschel's wisdom that touches your soul. Use that word to remind you of the possibility of deep Sabbath rest.

How Are You Called to Practice?

I hope you have discovered there is more to resting than taking a nap! We can learn to rest as we walk, integrating what are often experienced as two separate and opposite experiences. When you discover this art of moving restfully through your world, you might be able to say, as a directee of mine once exclaimed, "I am resting in my work."

Have you remembered some old messages from your family that inhibit your ability to practice rest? Are you willing to acknowledge the stories you were told and then make your own decision about resting? Honor your experiences of restful activities, and ask yourself if you might occasionally make these a priority in your busy life.

Biblical wisdom on rest can help us become more fully alive. We may rest as a way to prepare for our work, cooperating with the creative process. We may take the words of Rabbi Heschel to heart and discover for ourselves ways to rest in the gift of Sabbath, experiencing the deep peace and tranquility of *menuha*.

As you practice ways to rest, move slowly and tenderly, paying attention to what your body and soul need. Notice if you are comparing yourself to others, or whether you have let go of family "shoulds" only to substitute "shoulds" from this chapter such as: "I am exhausted. I should have rested more!" "I should move my resting to a deeper spiritual level." "I should find more restful activities." If you have done this, gently let these new "shoulds" go.

These ways to practice rest are not offered as a prescription. They are not designed to make you feel guilty. They are shared in the hope that you will, in your own time, find your way to a more fulfilling and restful life.

GUIDELINES FOR MORE EXTENDED PRACTICE

GRATEFUL BREATHING

- Turn your attention to your breath and simply notice how you are breathing. Notice the rhythm and how it feels in your body.

- Now breathe more deeply into your lungs and abdomen. Breathe in more and more and more until you are forced to exhale.

- Feel the release, the refreshment, before you breathe in again.

- If you are in a place where you can let out your breath with an audible sigh, do so. Maybe do that two or three times.

- Sighing is a spiritual practice!

- As I am practicing and writing, I am beginning to yawn. Although in our culture we tend to stifle our yawn, yawning is a message from the body to attend to our breath, to feel the life force within us.

- Allow your breath to return to normal and repeat the sequence two or three more times.

- In whatever way feels right for you, express gratefulness for the breath of life.

RESTING WHILE YOU WALK

You might wish to read this exercise through to get the suggestions in mind before you begin walking.

- Find a place outside where you can walk for at least two hundred yards.

- Begin by standing still. Pay attention to your breathing, allowing it to become calm and steady.

- Start walking, noticing if your movement feels like you are resting as you walk.

- Now speed up. Push yourself a little. Notice what happens to your breathing. Are you still resting as you walk?

- Return to an even pace and intentionally notice your surroundings. Do not judge them in any way; simply be present with all your senses as you walk. Are you resting as you walk?

- Shift your attention to a list of activities you have planned, a worry about someone you love, a fear about an upcoming event, or confusion about the state of the world. Are you resting as you walk while attending to these thoughts?

- Play with these different ways of walking a number of times. What feels best in your body and spirit?

- When you are ready, stop your movement, bring your mind back to the present moment, notice your breathing, and reflect on what you have experienced.

3

THE
PRACTICE
OF SILENCE

Finding Spaciousness, Stillness, and Inner Peace

Silence is never merely a cessation of words; it is not an absence, but the awareness of a presence.

John Chryssavgis

Many spiritual writers link the practices of silence and solitude, as if they automatically go together and you can't have one without the other. They experience solitude supporting silence, and silence infusing solitude. I agree with the wisdom that the practices of solitude and silence are intertwined, but I also believe there is much to be learned by exploring them separately.

Silence can be profound when practiced with others. The community can support and encourage silence; it can also illuminate the shadow sides of silence, making participants uncomfortable. The exploration of this discomfort can bear fruit.

The practice of solitude, whether silent or filled with music, reading, or technology, can uncover issues of loneliness that may need special attention. In this book I am therefore exploring the practices of silence and solitude in two separate chapters, while recognizing their deep connection. At the end of the next chapter on solitude, we will examine how linking these two practices, silence and solitude, might deepen the experience of both and possibly create a container for transformation.

Discovering Well-Being in Quiet Places

Silence is a way of waiting, a way of watching, and a way of listening to what is going on within and around us. Although the focus of this chapter is deep listening and inner quiet, we will begin by exploring external silence—that which is going on around us.

INVITATION TO PRACTICE

Stop reading for a moment and listen. What are the sounds you hear around you? Don't judge or label them; just notice.

I enjoyed silence long before I recognized it as a spiritual practice. As a child I liked being outside reading or alone in my room coloring or writing. Some evenings, after I was supposed to be in bed, I would silently sit on the stairs, listening to the soft voices of my parents talking. Although I loved to talk and would jabber nonstop in the morning, I found my own silence and the absence of noise comforting.

In my adult years I would seek out periods of silence by turning off the radio when alone in the car or stepping outside of a busy gathering to get away from the noisy chatter. Today, as I age, I recognize a growing need for longer periods of silence. The practice of external silence—not speaking and finding an absence of noise—is important for our physical, intellectual, and spiritual health. It is a necessary first step in the practice of silence. But that is not where we stop. What follows that first step is the much more difficult practice of attending to our inner quiet. The path between external and internal silence is listening.

Listening to Ourselves and Beyond Ourselves

Even when we intentionally seek out external silence, it is unlikely we will ever find a complete absence of noise. If we listen carefully, there will always be sounds that emerge from the silence. My office is very quiet, but at this moment in the middle of summer with the windows open, I can hear the sounds of a power mower, the barking of a neighbor's dog, a soft wind chime, my husband in the kitchen fixing lunch, and an infant next door crying. These noises are not distracting; rather they are comforting, for they are the familiar sounds of my home and neighborhood.

If I were to move from my computer to the soft chair in the corner to intentionally listen to my inner world, I know I would discover a cacophony of thoughts. The noise outside is nothing compared to what I hear within! If you have practiced some form of meditation or contemplative prayer, you will recognize this noisy inner world that I describe. Put your own stories into my descriptions of the process of listening for inner quiet. Notice what rings true for you and where your experiences differ from mine.

From my past practice of inner listening, I think I know what I will hear. My pattern of inner chatter is to make plans. I usually begin by planning what I will do when I stop "doing nothing." I may think about what to eat, when to take a walk, whose e-mail to respond to, or what book I might begin this evening. I might move further into the future and begin to plan a class I am to teach next month or wonder how large a suitcase I will need for my next trip.

As I listen to myself and recognize my thought patterns, I have a choice of how to respond to what I hear. I can get angry with myself for hearing the same old stuff and tell myself that I am a terrible listener. I can fall into despair, believing I will never discover true inner silence, and begin to wonder if I should give up this practice. Or I may simply notice my thoughts without judgment, maybe even with a little amusement, and allow myself to drop below my planning mind into a silent place within.

INVITATION TO PRACTICE
Put aside this book for a moment and close your
eyes. Listen to the sounds around you. Then turn your
attention to your inner world. What do you hear?
How do you respond to your inner noise?

When I discover that silent empty place, I might rest a moment, but soon my mind is busy again. Maybe I go back to planning, or I may replay an event in my mind, focusing on a confrontation with a friend, remembering what I said, what she said, how I felt, what I did, what I wished I'd done. I can spin this for quite a while as well. Then, as before, when I hear what I am doing, the pattern I am caught in, I notice without judgment and drop again beneath the chatter into that silent place where I can simply be present to what is.

This inner listening is the practice of listening to yourself. "What is the point?" you might ask. When we listen to what some Buddhists call "the monkey mind," we are able to observe our thoughts and discover the patterns that distract us from being fully present in any moment. The more we intentionally observe our thoughts, the more we become aware of how these thought patterns pull us away from being present to what is happening in our daily lives. As we see what we are doing, we can choose to interrupt those patterns and intentionally let go of our distracting thoughts rather than allowing them to lure us into elaborate scenarios. We simply see them and let them go by, like clouds in the sky or leaves floating on a quiet stream. This process of noticing and letting go, noticing and letting go, helps us develop a relative degree of interior silence. "It is unrealistic to aim at having no thoughts," writes Father Thomas Keating, teacher of Centering Prayer. "By interior silence we refer primarily to a state in which we do not become *attached* to the thoughts as they go by."[1]

For example, if I am on my way to a meeting and turn my attention to my thoughts, I may discover that once again I have become caught in planning. My mind is busy with what I will do when the meeting is over. Because my thoughts have taken over my consciousness, I am not aware of what is around me, and I am ignoring the slight feelings of anxiety about the coming interaction. When I notice what my mind is doing, I can turn my attention to my environment and my feelings. As I listen to myself and let the planning go, I realize that the day is blustery and cold and the people I pass all seem to be in a hurry just as I am, so I slow my pace and pay attention to my feelings. I realize I am not feeling anxious, but rather excited about the upcoming meeting. I have awakened to the present moment.

But the practice of listening must continue, for I may easily shift from the present moment to rehearsing how I would like the meeting to go. My thoughts may jump from deciding what I will say when I arrive, to wondering if people will engage, to anticipating difficult relationships, and then planning how I will handle conflict. Rehearsing a future event is such a common thought pattern for me that when I notice it once again, I simply say to myself, "Rehearsing." This inner word allows me to let those thoughts go and return to what is in the moment.

INVITATION TO PRACTICE
What are the most common thought patterns that take
you away from the present moment?

Practicing listening to ourselves in intentionally planned times of silence, or as we go about our daily lives, helps us find inner quiet and a deep stillness from which we may listen beyond ourselves. The mystics tell us that this silence creates space, an inner expansiveness that makes more room for God. Or the inner expansiveness becomes the experience of emptiness, not a frightening blank emptiness, but "emptiness dancing"[2]—a space filled with light and movement, with awareness and breath.

If you expect to hear a clear message coming from beyond yourself, from God or from the emptiness, I imagine you will be disappointed. Although a few people do hear a divine voice, all I hear when I am silent is more silence. It has taken me a long time to make peace with this reality. Expecting to hear something when I finally discovered moments of inner quiet, I blamed myself for hearing nothing. I was sure I was doing something wrong. Then I was sure that God did not find me worthy of a response. At times I wondered if God had gone missing.

Assurance came when I read a story about Mother Theresa of Calcutta. She was being interviewed and the reporter asked her, "Mother, when you pray, what do you say?" She replied, "Oh, I don't say anything, I just listen." The reporter then asked, "And what does God say?" She smiled slightly and responded, "He doesn't say anything, He just listens."

Simply listening is counterintuitive, for we think the purpose of listening is to hear something. We listen to music, we listen to speeches, we listen to friends and family, we listen to the news. But the practice of silence is really the practice of listening, being present to what is. In the silence, writes Quaker Patricia Loring, "it behooves us to listen with our hearts, the marrow of our bones, and our whole skin, as well as with our ears."[3]

Honoring Effortless Silence

I am aware that this exploration of silence and listening may sound like hard work. We need to focus and pay attention, first noticing our own inner noise, choosing to let the thoughts go, and dropping below them where we can listen intently to the silence. However, author and artist Jan L. Richardson suggests that focused attention is not the only avenue to listening and inner silence. She believes that sometimes wakefulness and awareness can come from a gap in our attention, a sleepy state, where we let go of all effort and simply embrace the mystery of being. This unfocused consciousness may be what happens when we slip into a hot bath after a long and stressful day, linger after dinner talking with family or friends, or go for an aimless walk in the moonlight. To help us recognize and honor those effortless moments, she offers us this blessing:

> *May you grow sleepy enough*
> *to find the gap where God lives.*
> *May your soul find its waking there.*[4]

Whether in focused attention or surrendering to the sleepiness, I no longer strain to hear something. Although I do not expect to receive a clear message, I do find that I am awakening and I am learning through my experiences of deep inner listening. I am learning to live more often in the present moment. I am learning the futility of judging myself and others. I am learning to embrace paradox. I am learning to find peace and stillness in the middle of a noisy, chaotic world. I am learning to allow all things to be as they are. These learnings can be summed up in the wise words of a little girl who wrote, "Silence reminds me to take my soul with me wherever I go."[5]

INVITATION TO PRACTICE
When have you experienced the spaciousness that comes from inner quiet? What have you been learning?

Practicing Silence in a Supportive Community

Although inner silence is usually practiced in solitude, listening can be enhanced when in the company of others who have made a covenant of silence and a commitment to deep listening. My first experience of intentional communal silence came in a weeklong retreat at the Shalem Institute for Spiritual Formation in Washington, D.C. After the first day of orientation, we began to honor silence. We had morning and evening teachings where we could interact with others around the content of the presentation. Brief worship services were held where we might chant and pray together. The rest of our time, including meals, was in silence. Most helpful in preparing for this time of quiet was the reminder that "it wasn't that we couldn't talk, rather, we didn't have to talk." Hearing those words made me realize that I had been approaching the upcoming silence as a rule to keep quiet, one imposed from above. With those gentle words, the burden of keeping silent was lifted and replaced with a sense of freedom.

Exploring the Shadow Side of Silence

When I started leading silent retreats, I realized that silence with others was not freeing for everyone. By talking with and learning from those who found silence frightening, I realized that people who have experienced forced silence or have been punished by the silence of another are very uncomfortable in a group setting with no conversation. These difficult experiences reveal the shadow side of silence.

I have heard many stories illustrating this struggle: The woman who had experienced domestic violence, who was reminded on a silent retreat of the years she spoke to no one of her abuse. The woman whose father had told her she had nothing of value to say. The man who remembered eating family meals in terrified silence as he and his brothers waited to see who would be the target of their father's anger. The man whose former wife used silence as a weapon in their relationship. People who have these experiences in their backgrounds do not embrace communal silence easily.

INVITATION TO PRACTICE

When have you been silenced by another person or a group of people? When do you silence yourself? When has silence been used as a weapon against you?

One of the most poignant stories I heard was from a woman on a five-day silent retreat. She came to me in tears the beginning of the second day. "No one is talking to me," she sobbed. "I'm feeling so left out." I reminded her that we had all made a covenant of silence and that no one was speaking to anyone. She was not being singled out. After sitting with her as she cried, she told me a story about how she had been the victim of a week of shunning while in high school. Her family had moved to a new city in the middle of her junior year. The girls of that school were in the habit of hazing new students with the cruel practice of shunning. If she approached a group, they would turn away and ignore her as if she weren't there. Students would look through her when she walked down the halls. For a week, none of her peers sought her out, talked to her, or listened to anything she had to say. She was isolated and terrifyingly alone.

As she came to the end of her story, I reminded her that her high school experience was *then*, and this retreat was *now*. She was among caring and like-minded people who had all agreed to be silent together. Maybe she could look to facial expressions and body language as she passed other retreatants on the path or when choosing a seat at lunch. I suggested that she look at others for clues of their welcome and kindness. She stayed for the full five days and at the end of the retreat expressed her gratitude for the healing of her memories. "I had no idea how deeply wounded I was by that one week twenty years ago," she told the group. "The silence we all chose to participate in and the kindness of this community have been truly life-giving."

Last year I was made aware of another manifestation of the shadow side of silence by Caran, a seminary student who wrote a reflection paper for one of my classes. "In the African-American church it is necessary to make the 'concerns' of the people audible and visible," she said. "As a culture, silence was forced upon us. In slavery we were silenced for asserting our right to be human. Moreover in order to survive, we had to silence ourselves."

In her desire to break the silence imposed on her people and herself, Caran decided to speak up. When she did, she discovered the difficulty in finding and expressing her voice in a white culture. When she spoke, she believed she was seldom heard. She sometimes felt she had to apologize for speaking or for speaking too long. "So I swallowed what I felt inside and did not let anything out of my tightened lips."

Caran understands the difference between forced silence that can deaden the body and soul and invoked silence that gives her the opportunity to breathe. "Every human has the right to speak and to be silent," she wrote. "Silence is not white, and vocalization is not to be equated with the African-American community. Both are necessary for wholeness."[6]

INVITATION TO PRACTICE
What insights or feelings are evoked in your mind and heart as you read Caran's thoughts and feelings?

Because of the healing that can occur in invoked or covenanted silence, I begin silent retreats with the invitation to explore the shadow sides of silence. By remembering and sharing, participants will not be as surprised by the feelings of fear, resentment, or resistance that are likely to emerge during the retreat. They might be willing to stay with the group rather than hiding in their rooms. They may discover that being silent together builds community.

A friend of mine watched her husband wave to a man on the other side of the street, then cross over to give him a hug. They didn't seem to say much to each other, and when he returned she asked him who that was. "I don't know his name," he said. "But I know him well. We've been together in a number of our yearly silent retreats for men."

When you are part of a silent community, you begin to know the other participants by listening to them with more than your ears. You notice body language—the way people hold themselves and how freely they move. You feel their hands as they reach out to touch you, and you notice their bodies if you hug. At table together, you might notice what other people are eating and become amused as you hear the noises made by chewing. If you take a silent walk with a friend, you can notice what she pays attention to or how fast or slowly he moves.

We often think speech connects us and conversation builds community, but talking can rupture relationships. An insensitive comment, an overly long monologue, an angry outburst, or an inappropriate question can cause us to close down or defend ourselves. Without the fear of distracting or hurtful words, we can become vulnerable and open. Sometimes tears flow freely; other times laughter bubbles forth. Individuals who gather together with the clear intention of allowing their external silence to support the inner silence of each person create a safe and trusting community.

Uncomfortable than relaxed

INVITATION TO PRACTICE
How do you think you would feel in a community of silence for one or two days? Fear? Relief? Bored? Safe?

Be Still and Know That I Am God

The wisdom expressed so clearly in the words of Psalm 46:10, "Be still and know that I am God," helps us understand that stillness is a quality of being. It is not something that we do, like being silent. It is something that we become. I believe that the practice of silence, like the practice of solitude we will explore in the next chapter, is the threshold that invites us into stillness. In fact, all the practices in this book have the potential of guiding us toward stillness. Think of the practice of caring for your body, how the body blessing might have led to stillness. Did the practice of resting—slowing down, breathing deeply, engaging in restful activities—lead you toward stillness? Keep the possibility of stillness alive as we explore practices in upcoming chapters. I have found all practices, even the most active ones, can help us recognize the stillness that lies within.

People often have a very narrow and distorted view of stillness. Did you ever play "statue" as a child? In this game, children hold hands, and the leader spins the line around until the child at the end is thrown off, to immediately freeze into the position in which he or she lands. This process is repeated until all the children are frozen, creating a sculpture garden. The frozen posture of a statue is what many people imagine when they think of stillness.

The true experience of stillness is vital and alive. Stillness has an energetic rhythm of its own. Our bodies have a variety of rhythms to choose from. We can flow through our lives, moving gracefully from one activity to another. We can move and stop, move and stop, thereby creating a sharp and jerky rhythm. Many times we combine these two rhythms into our own unique dance. Another way to move through life is on our tiptoes, always reaching up and out, or we might move close to the earth, feeling the comfort and support of the ground beneath our feet. Stillness, like all these other possible ways of moving, is a rhythm of life.

INVITATION TO PRACTICE

Move your hands and arms in each of these rhythms.
Let them flow, then change to jerky. Combine the two.
Reach up and out; reach down to the ground. Let your
hands rest in your lap. Which of these rhythms, or
combination of rhythms, are most familiar to you?

After the exercise suggested above, you may notice your hands tingling when they come to stillness after moving in these other rhythms. They are at rest and at peace even as they contain a lively energy. Such is the rhythm of stillness. People who have discovered stillness can be very active and involved in the world. However, their activities do not appear frantic or driven, but rather come from a deep well of presence and peace.

No one lives from stillness all the time, but recognizing that it is an essential part of our being allows us to choose it more and more often. When you realize you are rushing from appointment to appointment, you slow down and remember another way to be. If you become aware of how you live most of your life on your toes, you might find a way to ground yourself in the present moment. If you seem to flow from one thing to another—graceful, but in perpetual motion—try stopping for a moment and become aware of the tingle and liveliness of a moment of stillness.

Looking around at people and nature, you will discover how all these rhythms are being lived out. Notice runners who seem to float along the track as if with no effort. Watch your neighbor who leaves his house only to return for something he has forgotten, and then returns again, and maybe once again, before he finally leaves. Pay attention to the birds that are mostly moving up and out and away, and the fox that moves close to the ground. Look at a tree. It has been said that if we sit next to a tree and feel its life force, it will teach us all we need to know about stillness.

INVITATION TO PRACTICE
Find a tree you can sit beside and lean against it, if that is possible. What do you learn about stillness?

How Are You Called to Practice?

Although we moved quickly from the practice of finding and creating exterior silence to the practice of listening, do not underestimate the power of regular periods of external silence. You might embrace the moments of silence that appear at home, at work, or in the wider community, avoiding the urge to fill them with phone calls, music, or the Internet. You might plan for times of silence, scheduling them into your day. Could you get up five minutes earlier than usual to have the quiet house to yourself, or close the door to your office and simply gaze at a beloved object or look out the window? If we pay attention and listen, more silence is available to us than we imagine.

Are you interested in listening to yourself and beyond yourself? Don't be surprised if you feel afraid of this practice. Most of us like our familiar patterns of thought, even if they are not helpful. By listening, you may receive insights that could call you to change. Approach this practice with an attitude of curiosity, as a child examines a newly found object.

It is not easy for me to engage in inner listening on my own. I need others to help me hold the silent space and keep me from running away. Much of my deepest inner listening occurs with my spiritual director, a practice I will explore in more depth in chapter 6. I also seek out groups that include contemplative prayer as part of their schedule, as well as attend silent retreats. The need for companionship in the silence may be your need as well. If so, look for a group that practices silence that you might wish to join.

Do not forget Jan Richardson's advice that focus is not the only way to listen. Relish the sleepy moments in your life, the gaps where you might not even realize you are listening but you know soon after that something subtle occurred because you feel more spacious and at peace.

At any moment, and in any situation, you can watch and listen for stillness in others, in nature, and in yourself. You don't need to practice stillness so much as recognize it. Waiting in a doctor's office, you realize you are not anxious or agitated, not filling up the time with old magazines, but rather you are still. Watching your child at play, you recognize the quality of stillness in his little body and his focused attention. When sitting with a quiet friend, you sense her stillness and do not fill the space with chatter. A bird swoops by and lands on a nearby branch—alert and still for a moment before it silently flies away.

Any way that you choose to practice silence in your life will assist the waking up process and guide you to more fullness of life.

GUIDELINES FOR MORE EXTENDED PRACTICE

A VARIETY OF MEDITATION AND CONTEMPLATIVE PRAYER PRACTICES

Many methods of meditation and contemplative prayer to be practiced in silence are available to us in the literature of different spiritual traditions. Some of the practices have been taught for centuries, and others are new variations on old themes. I will describe a few simple practices for you to explore. Approach them with an attitude of experimentation, not worrying about doing any of them "right." Play with the ones that attract you, and see if you think practicing any one method consistently might strengthen your inner listening and guide you toward spaciousness, stillness, and inner peace.

For each practice you decide to engage, begin by finding a place where you will not be interrupted, and take some time for preparation by attending to what is happening in your body, feelings, and mind. Many practitioners recommend you sit in an upright position in a chair or on the floor; however, some people will meditate or pray lying down, walking, or even swimming.

BREATH COUNTING

Counting your breath is a way to focus your attention in the present moment while giving your mind something to do. As you draw your attention to your breathing, begin counting your inhalations, slowly and deliberately, one through ten, and then start over. You probably won't get to ten before your mind wanders away. That's all right, just notice that you have lost your focus, let go of the distractions, and start counting again at one. This patient acceptance of losing your way and starting over is helpful in learning to accept this process as a way of life.

Although you may begin breath counting in order to relax, you will likely find that the practice takes great effort and can become frustrating. If you are able to stay with this practice over time, you may become more aware of your breathing in the middle of your life, and the attention to your breathing will extend to other aspects of your inner life, such as your thoughts and feelings.

CENTERING PRAYER

Originating in twelfth-century Christianity and reintroduced to the modern world by Father Thomas Keating, Centering Prayer is a method of prayer that guides you into the presence of God. You begin this practice by selecting a prayer word, sometimes called a sacred word, to remind you of your intention to simply rest silently in the Presence. Saying the word to yourself at the beginning of the prayer time indicates your consent to enter fully into the experience. As you do so, notice when your attention shifts to other things—thoughts, feelings, physical sensations. As you realize that your mind has carried you away, say your word to remind you of your intention to simply be in the holy Presence.

Centering Prayer is a method of intention, not attention. The sacred word is not used repetitively to focus your attention. A mantra, a word or phrase said silently over and over, is used for that purpose. If you find it necessary to use your prayer word many, many times in a twenty-minute session, your prayer word may feel like a mantra. Do not be discouraged if that happens. The story has been told about Father Keating's response to a woman complaining to him that she was so distracted during prayer that she must have used her sacred word a hundred times: "How wonderful! You returned to God one hundred times! What could be better than that?"

TRUE MEDITATION

Spiritual writer and teacher Adyashanti describes true meditation as simply allowing everything to be as it is. Rather than doing battle with the mind to meditate correctly, he invites you to move from trying to perfect a technique to letting go of any technique. Most techniques are designed to control and manipulate the mind to reach a desired outcome—clarity, peace, enlightenment. Only by letting the techniques fall away can you discover your natural state of being.

The natural state of consciousness is peaceful and still, filled with deep wisdom and deep knowing. They are at the essence of who you are. You do not need to work toward this natural state; all you have to do is notice it and give yourself to it. "To sit down and let everything be as it already is," Adyashanti writes, "to let go of control and to let go of manipulation—is itself a very deep act of faith."[7]

True meditation is effortless, not in the way of being lazy or uncaring, but rather having just enough effort to be in the moment and to be present to what is. As you practice allowing everything to be as it is in silent meditation, you will begin to notice that you carry this way of being into your life. You allow the weather to be just as it is. You allow the repairs on your home to proceed just as they are. You allow your childhood to be just as it was. I have found practicing in the midst of life to be one way to begin the practice of true meditation—going from off-cushion to a more intentional on-cushion practice.

4

THE
PRACTICE
OF SOLITUDE
Making Friends with Yourself

Solitude is a means to an end, not an end in itself. It brings us things nobody else can give us.

Lionel Fisher

Every summer for almost twenty years I have gone to a small house, high in the Rocky Mountains, for my annual five-day solitary retreat. I make this annual retreat to immerse myself in creation, learning what nature can teach me about stillness. All alone, my activities are guided by my own rhythms—eating when I am hungry, sleeping when I am tired, walking when my body says, "Move." I may sit for hours watching the birds come and go at the feeders, or leave the cabin before breakfast for an early-morning walk.

My retreats are not silent in the purest sense, for although I have no phone, no Internet connection, no music, no TV, I do read and write. Sometimes I enjoy talking to the animals—greeting the birds as they fly close to the window, telling the deer how beautiful they are.

This may sound idyllic, but being on retreat alone is disorienting. My usual patterns are no longer there. Every moment becomes a choice. Looking back over my journals from the early years, I notice how I tried to ease my discomfort by quantifying everything I did. I recorded the books I read, the hours I slept, the miles I walked. I needed to have a definitive answer to the question of others, "What did you do for five days alone?" I no longer record my activities, although I make notes of dreams, of wildlife sightings, and of weather conditions. Now, when people ask, I respond, "A little of everything, a lot of nothing."

Although my patterns on retreat have changed, I still become anxious as I leave home, for I have no idea what will happen. With nothing external to structure my time—what will I do? With no one defining me—who will I be? With the space and time to listen—what will I hear? Sometimes my fears grow to the point that I seriously consider canceling my retreat, but each year I pack my bags and go in search of solitude.

The practice of solitude allows me to listen and to see with the ears and eyes of the heart. Alone, without external distractions, thoughts and feelings spontaneously arise to be explored. Maybe a long-forgotten dream returns with a pertinent message. Grief over a broken relationship may need to be revisited. Benedictine nun Joan Chittister describes the effects of solitude as bringing "the raw material of life to the surface of our souls. It turns an inner light on the external chaos of our lives and requires us to come to grips with it."[1]

Over the years, as I have struggled to come to grips with what emerges, I have found myself judging and evaluating my retreats. One year I got an insight into my personality that helped me shift some problematic behaviors. That was a "good" retreat. Another year I had a series of nightmares. That was a "hard" retreat. Writing a few letters asking others for forgiveness allowed me to think I'd had a "productive" retreat. Then one year I had a retreat during which nothing happened. Nothing surfaced, no breakthroughs, no dramatic weather, no dreams—just ordinary time. Weeks after I returned I realized that what had happened was that "nothing happened." My disappointment with the ordinary (what I tend to evaluate as "boring") brought me face-to-face with my need for drama. I look back at that retreat

with gratitude, for it taught me that what is important in seeking time
alone is not the experience itself, but what I am able to learn.

My yearly solitary retreats have become more about being than
doing. They teach me patience and are helping me cultivate an inner
solitude. I practice being alone with myself so I can find my way to
being alone even in the midst of others.

INVITATION TO PRACTICE

Pause in your reading, and recognize that no matter what is
happening around you, you are alone. If you are willing, say
aloud or silently, "Here and now I am alone with myself."

This past year my retreat felt a little different, for I went to the
mountains with the intention to use some of my retreat time for writing.
In the past, I have avoided having any agenda, but this year it seemed a
good idea to write about solitude while in the middle of a solitary experience. That felt exciting, and I even began composing the first sentence
of this chapter as I drove the two and a half hours to my destination.

After arriving and settling in, I thought about opening my computer and plugging it in so as to be ready to start writing. But I
didn't. I wandered from window to window, sat gazing at the mountains in a reclining chair, found a jigsaw puzzle and poured out the
pieces, ate a handful of nuts, glanced through a few of the books I
had brought. I was unable to settle down. "Oh, well," I thought. "I'll
write tomorrow."

I awoke early the next morning and lay in bed thinking about my
morning of meditation and writing. But when I arose and had fixed
my first cup of tea, I went back to my chair, watched the activity and
the beauty outside my window, read a few pages, fixed another cup of
tea, then worked a little on the puzzle. This pattern continued for the
rest of the day. I realized the organic rhythm of retreat had defeated
my plans for productivity that I had carried into this mysterious place

and time. I saw that yielding to being did not mean I had stopped being useful and productive. Rather, my work and my words could come from another place—freer and more creative, less driven by outcome. I laughed at myself for having once again tried to structure the mystery, and I sighed a prayer of gratitude for having been caught.

INVITATION TO PRACTICE
When have you become aware that your agenda had yielded to another way of being in the world? What was that like? Can you say thank you?

Facing the Dragon of Loneliness

When I teach about the practice of solitude, I am often asked about experiences of loneliness. I imagine some of you have been holding similar questions in your hearts, for hidden behind the possibility of a deep and joyful solitude is the fear of abandonment and isolation or maybe of old memories of lonely times. If you are to engage the practice of solitude, these concerns need to be addressed, just as we examined the shadow sides of silence in the previous chapter. "Our language has wisely sensed the two sides of being alone," writes theologian Paul Tillich. "It has created the word loneliness to express the pain of being alone. And it has created the word solitude to express the glory of being alone."[2]

Loneliness is a human condition; it will never leave us. We can embrace this reality, or we can fight against it. When we encounter this existential loneliness, we often have feelings of sadness and a sense of isolation and seek to find ways to feel better. If we are able to accept that we are simply alone, that nothing is wrong and there is nothing to fix, we are on our way to embracing solitude. In our religious and secular cultures, we usually defend against loneliness by seeking others to fill the void we are experiencing or by distracting ourselves with busyness. If this has been your pattern of coping with loneliness, you know that it may work for a while, but never for long. We are disappointed when the new friend or lover doesn't make the loneliness go away. We find a new community and join it wholeheartedly, hoping it will ease our pain, and we become disillusioned when we find we are still lonely in the midst of gatherings. A host of new activities might mask our loneliness, but soon we realize that what we are doing is purposeless and is just making us tired. We may then realize that the only way to ease our loneliness is to face it and experience the feelings, as difficult as that may seem.

INVITATION TO PRACTICE
Are you feeling lonely right now? When did you last feel lonely? What did you do with your lonely feelings?

When we don't run away from our loneliness, we may find in it a clue to what we truly are longing for. When we embrace our loneliness, we may discover possibilities for new life. To live life fully "we must first find the courage to enter into the desert of our loneliness and to change it by gentle and persistent effort into a garden of solitude," writes spiritual teacher Henri J. M. Nouwen.[3]

I believe the persistent effort he calls us to is not striving to solve the problem of our loneliness, not trying to figure out why we are lonely, and not running away. Rather, it is the practice of staying still, sitting with the feelings, listening attentively to our own struggles so we are able to find answers in our own hearts.

One evening in the days leading up to Christmas, I began to weep. My tears were different from the times when my crying was a natural response to pain, either physical or emotional. They were not the tears I have shed in compassion and solidarity with the struggles of others and the world. These tears seemed to have no reason, but when Jim asked me what was wrong, I replied, "I'm lonely."

My response startled me, for it didn't make sense. My family was gathering for the holidays. I had been catching up with old friends via cards and e-mails. We had attended some lovely parties. We had plans for New Year's. How could I be lonely? My first thought was that I was missing my two dearest friends, who lived far away. Maybe I should call them? Then I wondered if Jim and I needed more time alone together. But that didn't fit. His retirement gave us many good hours and days together. Then the truth behind my dilemma bubbled up and out. "I need to be alone," I cried. "All this togetherness! I am lonely for myself!"

How irrational! How counterintuitive! If I am lonely, it doesn't make sense for me to want to be alone. But I discovered the opposite to be true. When I made the effort to face my loneliness, the hope-lessness I experienced became a threshold to new life. I recognized and honored my need for solitude. I found ways to meet that need by taking a morning alone and an evening by myself. I was able to enter into the Christmas festivities with a lighter heart. From the time in my garden of solitude, I discovered new ways to interact and to be content in our family gatherings.

Nouwen affirms my experience of the deep connection between solitude and a rich community or family life. He believes that although talking, working, and playing together may draw us closer together, "these interactions derive their fruit from solitude…. In solitude we discover each other in a way that physical presence makes difficult if not impossible. There we recognize a bond with each other that does not depend on words, gestures, or actions, a bond much deeper than our own efforts can create."[4]

Early Experiences of Being Alone: Avoided or Encouraged?

There is a common belief that introverts are more comfortable with the practice of solitude than are extroverts. To some extent, that may be true, but there are other factors to be considered. Psychotherapist and writer Anthony Storr believes that the capacity to be alone is learned in early childhood regardless of temperament.

In collaboration with his colleague Donald Winnicott, Storr theorizes that infants with a secure attachment to a mother figure become able to be alone in the presence of the mother. By this he means that when the basic needs of the infants have been satisfied, they no longer need the mother to define their identity, and they are free to discover who they are. Once the infants have learned to be alone in the presence of others, they can begin to be comfortably alone with no one else around. This early practice—alone with others and then alone by oneself—helps older children and adults develop the capacity to be comfortable without the presence of others. Storr admonishes parents to give their children time and opportunity for solitude.[5]

Years ago, soon after reading Storr's material, I found myself in a gathering of women on an outdoor patio. As we talked and laughed and sipped tea, I noticed one woman's young daughter not far away in the garden playing by herself. I remember thinking that this was what Storr had described, a child happily alone in the presence of others. But the girl's mother did not seem to see the beauty of what was happening, for she kept calling to her, "Susie, come here and be with us. You don't have to be alone. Come on Susie, we would like you here with us."

INVITATION TO PRACTICE
What do you remember about being given the
opportunity to be alone as a child? Was anything said or
done to discourage solitude?

As a young child I was given permission and encouragement to be alone. I loved riding my bike by myself throughout the neighborhood. I liked playing solitaire, coloring, and doing puzzles. In the summer I would spend hours at the children's library reading in their "secret garden." Our family would often read in the evenings, each with his or her own book, happily alone together.

As a teenager, my mother became concerned about my solitary nature. She began encouraging me to have friends over after school, to accept party invitations, to go in groups to school events. I began to feel there was something wrong with the pleasure I found in being alone. In spite of these conflicting feelings, I continued to search out solitude as an adult. Even though I lived alone after my divorce, I loved going backpacking for a few days with only my dog for company. I found small cabins in remote places to rent while exploring new territory—in my inner life as well as the world.

Often people near and dear to us do not understand or encourage the practice of solitude. Soon after my marriage to Jim, I remember my mother saying to me, "Now that you are married with a family, I don't imagine you will be going off by yourself anymore." To which I replied, "Oh, Mother, I will probably go more often. All this togetherness is exhausting." There was a stunned silence on the other end of the phone before she offered a warning. "Well," she huffed, "I just hope you don't ruin your marriage by running off by yourself."

My younger stepson Paul didn't want me to go off by myself either, but for a very different reason; he wanted to go with me. "I'll be really, really quiet and really good. Please, please let me go with you." He didn't understand that my leaving was not to get away from him, which is what I think he feared, but that I was going toward something that required my being alone. He finally made peace with his stepmother's oddness when I told him that his father was not allowed to accompany me either. With great relief he said, "I thought Dad didn't go because he had to stay home and take care of us. I didn't know you didn't want him either!"

INVITATION TO PRACTICE
Are there people in your life who object to your practice
of solitude? How might you help them to understand?

The Journey Is the Destination:
Walking Nowhere Alone

The practice of solitude does not require a retreat or dedicated time away. In fact, developing the ability to find solitude in everyday life is an important part of the spiritual practice. In *The Sign of Jonas*, Thomas Merton describes solitude as "not something you must hope for in the future. Rather it is a deepening of the present, and unless you look for it in the present you will never find it."[6]

When I'm not off on retreat, walking alone is one way I practice solitude on a daily basis. I walk to clear my head. I walk to get out into the world. I walk to prepare my body for an upcoming hiking trip. Often I walk the same route—out the door, turn left to the parkway, continue on around the park, back to the avenue, and home. Sometimes I stride out smartly, then slow down and wander, looking at the flowers in the summer, watching for patches of ice in the winter.

I am not going anywhere. I have no destination, no goal. I feel like I am living out the words of poet Antonio Machado: "Traveler, there is no path; paths are made by walking."[7] Although I sometimes enjoy walking with others, finding a regular walking partner or joining a hiking group has no appeal. I want time and space to be alone with myself. I don't listen to music or tapes. I listen to the world in which I live. I delight at the sounds of children's laughter. I flinch at the squeal of brakes. I say good morning to the elderly gentleman who always tips his hat to me in reply. I marvel at the colors and the shapes along the way, and I wonder why a certain house is so neglected.

When I practice silence in my solitary walks, I also listen to my inner life. I attend to my feelings and honor them even as I try to understand them. I notice the way my mind goes in habitual patterns, and when possible I slow it down or change tracks. Sometimes I am delighted by the sudden appearance of a new idea or the solution to a problem I have been holding close.

INVITATION TO PRACTICE
Put down the book and walk around your house, or
down the walk, or around the block. What is it like to
walk for the sake of walking?

A number of years ago I discovered walking meditation when I attended a daylong retreat with Buddhist monk and peace activist Thich Nhat Hanh. It was held in the gym at the University of Colorado, and more than a thousand people arrived to hear him.

After twenty minutes of sitting meditation and a brief talk, Thich Nhat Hanh's assistant told us we were going to practice walking meditation. I immediately had unpleasant images of a thousand people walking around and around the gym, but he surprised me. The crowd was divided into ten or fifteen groups, each with a leader. We were instructed to silently find our guide, form a line, and follow him outside. Suddenly we were walking nowhere together, slowing down, noticing our breathing, and paying attention to our feet touching the earth.

As our small group wandered the hilly campus, I saw the other groups in the distance, moving slowly going nowhere. I was filled with wonder at how solitude and silence were creating community. I don't remember a thing Thich Nhat Hanh said that day, but the experience of walking nowhere together lingers in my soul.

Buddhism is not the only tradition in which walking is a spiritual practice. Christians walk the Stations of the Cross. Muslims walk round and round the Kaaba in Mecca. In the secular world, many individuals claim solitary walking as their spiritual practice. "Thomas Huxley … considered his mountain jaunts 'the equivalent of churchgoing'; Henry Thoreau called his early-morning walks 'a blessing for the whole day'; and the travel writer Bruce Chatwin wrote that 'walking is not a path to God, it *is* God.'"[8]

INVITATION TO PRACTICE
What longings, if any, do these descriptions of solitary
walking practices stir in your soul?

The Capacity to Be Alone: Self-Discovery, Creativity, and Intimacy

Solitary walking often leads to self-discovery. Self-discovery is not the same as self-realization. We may hope that if we learn to spend time in solitude we will wake up to who we truly are—all distortions stripped away to discover our deepest essence. Self-realization may come as grace, but not usually before the long hard work of self-discovery. The process of self-discovery includes seeing what we have been hiding from, recognizing unrealized potential, and becoming aware of the changes we must make to become truly alive.

It was not fun on retreat to face my addictive need to be productive. It was not easy to admit that I had a high need for drama, and if it didn't appear I would create it. Steeped in the practice of solitude, it was humbling to realize how lonely I still could be. I didn't like seeing how attached I get to my plans, trying to control outcomes, not only on retreat but in other parts of my life as well. The good news is, there is great relief in facing what we have been afraid of or hiding from. With things out in the open, new ways of being and behaving appear. New possibilities often give birth to liveliness and a lightness of spirit. Our deserts of loneliness may turn slowly into gardens of solitude as we develop the capacity to be alone.

INVITATION TO PRACTICE
When have you faced a truth about yourself that was
not easy to see but led to growth and new possibilities?

Self-discovery and possible self-realization are not the only fruits of the practice of solitude. Often in our solitude we tap into depths of creativity we had not before recognized. Although creative people may need others in the beginning stages of their work, many of them recognize that the final resolution happens in solitude. This is true for those who invent new products, for innovative thinkers in all fields, and for artists of all stripes.

Although history bears out the correlation between the capacity for solitude and creativity, modern culture has been going in the opposite direction. Many of our schools and classrooms, from elementary school through college and into graduate degree programs, have become open spaces where interaction is a high priority and group-learning activities are the norm. Students of any age are often discouraged from working on projects alone.

INVITATION TO PRACTICE
How do you learn best?
How much interaction do you need?
How much solitude?

Businesses that have followed this same idea are discovering that although this is a stimulating work environment for some, other employees are tired of the noise and the lack of privacy in open workspaces. They complain they are often interrupted, find it hard to concentrate, and feel stress at the end of the day. Some are now requesting offices with doors that close. They want to be able to work alone, without the constant pressure to interact.

I think that organizations and institutions fear that individuals learning and working on their own will become isolated or competitive, losing sight of the bigger picture. But what seems to be true is that people who do their best work alone are eager to share it. They don't want to isolate themselves; they simply know they are able to be much more creative in solitude and will ultimately have more to contribute.

Religious leaders—Moses, Jesus, Muhammad, and Buddha—as well as the lesser-known saints, prophets, monks, and shamans, have always gone off alone to discover wisdom they later shared. Moses was alone while leading the flock of sheep belonging to his father-in-law beyond the wilderness to Horeb, the mountain of God. God appeared to Moses in a burning bush and then instructed him to go to his people and deliver them from slavery in Egypt (Exodus 3).

During his busy ministry, Jesus went off alone to renew and refresh his spirit. "In the morning, while it was still very dark, he got up and went out to a deserted place, and there he prayed" (Mark 1:35). He would then return to the crowds awaiting his teaching and healing. Muhammad went regularly to a cave on Mount Hira. Here the Prophet received a revelation from God, which became the first verse of the Holy Qur'an. This revelation led him back to his people. And, according to the sacred texts, the Buddha received enlightenment alone, under the bodhi tree, leading him to a life of teaching and compassion.

And so it is for us today. The practice of solitude will not necessarily lead you into isolation, but rather, may allow you to approach the world with a solitude of heart, an inner attitude that frees you from looking to others to make you whole, to take away your loneliness, or to tell you who you are. With a solitary heart you will be able to interact more authentically and bring your whole self to your family and your community.

An inner quality of solitude is what allows intimacy to deepen with a loved one. This happens slowly when both people are willing to face their own loneliness, enter willingly into the process of self-discovery, and honor the solitude of themselves and the other. The poet Kahlil Gibran captures the beauty of this intimacy when he likens it to the strings of a lute that are separate but quiver with the same music.[9]

INVITATION TO PRACTICE
How have you experienced solitude deepening
intimacy? Is there a relationship in your life that might
grow deeper by the practice of solitude?

Silence and Solitude Together: A Furnace of Transformation

As we explored silence and solitude separately, I am sure you saw shades of solitude in the practice of silence and heard echoes of silence in the practice of solitude. Practicing moments of solitude in your car, on a walk, or on your front porch, you may have been silent, listening to the sounds around you and the thoughts and feelings within. While practicing the watching, waiting, and listening of silence, you may have been alone or somewhat apart from others. Through these experiences you have already had a taste of silence and solitude simultaneously. What might it be like to intentionally practice them together?

The Desert Fathers and Mothers of third- and fourth-century Christianity can be our guides for this practice. They were called into the Egyptian desert to come face-to-face with God and with themselves, thus testing and studying what it meant to be fully human. They aimed to live a life that reflected a reversal of all the ordinary social values and expectations of their time.

For these early hermits, the desert was a barren place. Vegetation was scarce and the environment challenging. They were alone, with no place to hide and no one to blame; there was no room for lying or deceit. The Desert Fathers and Mothers could only face up to themselves—their temptations, their attachments, their deepest desires, and their own deaths. This brutally honest accounting smashed old beliefs and old ways of seeing—everything they knew and thought was true.

Many of the stories from this period tell of the abundance of tears shed in the desert. The hermits understood their tears to signify a softening of the soul, clarity of the mind, and an opening to new life. Tears confirmed their readiness to allow their hearts to be broken and their lives to come apart, so as to be free to be reborn into a world of healing.[10]

This desert practice of the early centuries is not likely one that we aspire to. However, many of us have been through a desert, those times when we find ourselves alone, with no place to hide and with nothing to do except wait, watch, and listen while we face ourselves. I think of my divorce and how I felt set apart and lonely; how I silenced myself in my pain. I had to face the end of all I had believed to be true, and look closely at my participation in the ending of my marriage and my attachment to cultural expectations. Facing my demons made new life possible.

When my father died suddenly at age sixty, I was pulled through another desert. My world turned upside down, there was no firm place to stand and nothing seemed real. My heart was broken, but my soul was softened. After a long time of grieving, I was able to face the future with a new understanding of the amazing gift of every moment.

Right now I am in the middle of a different kind of desert. As I mentioned in the introduction, I am realizing that although I still claim my Christian roots and identity, I have let go of many of the teachings of traditional Christianity. I have had to look carefully at each belief, sorting through what is true for me and what needs to be discarded. My old images of God have disappeared, and my habitual ways of seeing the world have changed. It is a lonely place to be, but at the same time I feel deeply connected. I see options before unrecognized, and I feel the promise of liberation.

INVITATION TO PRACTICE
When have you been in the desert? What were the
terrors, and what were the gifts?

We do not need to seek out the desert. The desert will come to us. Our smaller, quieter, less dramatic practices of silence and solitude will help us navigate the journey through the wasteland: knowing how to be still and listen, knowing how to face our own loneliness. Welcoming our tears, knowing they will cleanse our minds and hearts and will soften our souls, will give us the strength to go on to new life. Transformation does not only happen in one journey to the desert—in one large furnace. The possibility of transformation is present in every moment. We simply need to be still and notice the opportunities as they arise, for arise they will!

How Are You Called to Practice?

If you live alone or are alone much of the time, the last thing you may want is more time to yourself. You might be more interested in joining others for spiritual practices or feel called to acts of service. However, you could spend some time reflecting on whether your time alone is defined by loneliness or by solitude. If there is loneliness you have not faced, that might be a place to begin.

For those of you longing for solitude, this practice can become part of everyday life. In most people's lives, there will be times when you find yourself alone. You may be in your car, either speeding along or stuck in traffic. Your friend is late for your lunch date, and you sit alone in the restaurant. You become aware that your teenagers are in their rooms and you are alone in the kitchen. We often don't notice these times as opportunities for spiritual practice. I find it helpful to say to myself, "I am alone," then appreciate the moment without reaching for my e-mail or the phone or otherwise distracting myself from the experience of solitude.

You may wish to plan some solitary time for yourself. Begin with a few hours or a half a day. Take a book and go to the park. Go see a movie by yourself. Let your family know that you would like an hour by yourself on the porch. As you practice solitude in this way, you will discover how the people around you respond to this practice.

This information will help you negotiate longer periods of solitude, if you decide that is what your soul desires.

By approaching the practice of solitude slowly, you will begin to notice if you are afraid of being alone. You can then explore those fears in a safe place so you won't be surprised when away by yourself. One of the extended practices is designed to help you look gently at your experience of loneliness.

Spending more time looking back at your experiences of desert spirituality could guide you toward the practices you might need in another journey through the desert. Pay attention to what was helpful in past encounters, and become aware of what other ways of being could assist you in the future. What practices might provide you strength, courage, and hope?

GUIDELINES FOR MORE EXTENDED PRACTICE

EXPLORING YOUR EXPERIENCES OF LONELINESS

- Find a place where you can be alone for about thirty minutes. You may wish to have a journal with you or some other writing material.

- Take a moment to quiet yourself, using your breath and paying attention to your body, feelings, and mind.

- When you are ready, bring into mind and heart a time of loneliness in your life. It might be in your childhood, or you might be in the middle of it now.

- Remember and experience the context of that time. Where were you? What was going on in your life? Who was with you, and who was absent?

- As you experience the loneliness of that time, see if you can locate the feeling in your body. What other feelings were part of the lonely experience—grief, physical pain, fear?

➥ Remember what you did with those lonely feelings. Are you willing to accept the ways you responded to loneliness at that time of your life?

➥ Imagine now that the man or woman you are today can reach out and embrace your lonely self. How does that feel? What words of comfort or assurance might you offer to the lonely child, adolescent, or young adult?

➥ If you are experiencing loneliness in your life right now, imagine you have a wise and loving self within who can embrace you. Hear and receive the words of assurance that you are given.

➥ When you have experienced all you need at this moment in time, allow the images to fade, and bring your attention back to the present.

➥ Reflect on, and maybe write about, what it would mean in your life to not run from your loneliness or try to fix it, but rather to accept your loneliness so that it might turn into a garden of solitude.

WALKING MEDITATION: SLOWLY GOING NOWHERE

The purpose of walking meditation is to still the mind, become present to the moment, and celebrate the wonder of the earth on which we walk. Walking meditation is not just for our own peace of mind, but to spread peace throughout the world. I have adapted Thich Nhat Hanh's guidance on walking meditation for this specific practice.

➥ Find somewhere you can walk for about fifteen minutes. Look for a place that is fairly level and easy to walk along. It could be outside in a park or around a few blocks. Indoors, look for a room that you can walk comfortably around or across.

➥ As you stand to begin your walk, feel your feet on the ground while you attend to your breathing.

- You might want to set an intention for this walk, such as "I am walking for peace" or "I bring gentle steps to a hurting world."

- Walk slowly and intentionally, putting your heel down first and feeling the full length of your foot along the ground before you pick up the other foot and proceed.

- You may feel a little off-balance at first, and if that happens, right yourself and continue on.

- To focus more on the wonder of your walking and the beauty of the earth, you might want to imagine that each step is planting a flower or that every time you lift your foot you are causing a light and healing breeze.

- Place a gentle smile on your face, allowing that expression to resonate within and bring forth a feeling of contentment.

- When you are able to walk gently and easily, your mind may begin to wander. Bring it back to each step, feeling the touch of your feet on the ground that supports you.

- Remember, you are walking with no goal or destination. No need to hurry. Just be where you are.

- When your walk is over, stand still for a moment. You may wish to bow to the path as an expression of your gratefulness for being so fully present to what is.

5

THE
PRACTICE
OF LETTING GO

Releasing Your Attachments, Your Past, and Your Future

We must let go of the life we have planned so as to accept the life that is waiting for us.

Joseph Campbell

Imagine a trapeze artist walking across the sawdust floor of a circus tent. She walks purposefully and gracefully toward the rope ladder leading to a tiny platform high above. Slowly she begins to climb, the ladder swaying as she ascends. Upon reaching the platform, she grasps the bar attached to another rope secured to the top of the tent. Poised on the edge of the platform, she pushes off into the air, swinging forward and back, gaining speed.

At the same time, across from her, another artist holds his bar, steps off his platform, and begins to swing, soon matching the rhythm of his partner. With fluid movements, he twists his body up and over the bar to hang by his knees. With his arms free, you realize he has become the "catcher," ready and waiting for her to let go. Back and forth they swing as the tension mounts. Suddenly she releases her bar and is flying through the air. In that brief moment she experiences the profound freedom of letting go.

INVITATION TO PRACTICE
Tighten your hands into fists, imagining you are clutching
something as tightly as the trapeze artist held on to her bar.
Then open your hands, letting go of whatever you are holding.
Experience the release in your body, breath, and spirit.

In the Buddhist tradition, the slogan "nothing to hold on to" is understood to be at the heart of spiritual practice. When we try to hold on to anything, we are denying the reality of impermanence. Even though we know intellectually that everything is changing, we search for ways to avoid this truth. We expend enormous amounts of energy seeking permanence and security, looking for ways to keep things as they are. We hold on.

Imagine what would happen to the trapeze artist if she didn't let go. She would swing indefinitely, stuck in the one back-and-forth movement, just one way of being alive. She must let go to free herself for new life. And so it is for us. Letting go is a spiritual practice that offers freedom and space to grow and change, cooperating with our impermanent reality rather than fighting against it.

Letting Go of Material Things

Letting go is a life practice to be experienced in many different ways. One way to begin practicing is by letting go of material things, in order to experience the release and freedom that comes when we don't hold on.

Take a look around you at all the things you possess. Unless you are living in a one-room studio apartment, what you can see from your chair is probably not everything you own. What fills other rooms, closets, basements, and attics? What about your garage or a storage unit? Where did all these things come from?

When my husband retired, first on his agenda was to clean out the basement and the garage. He felt weighted down by all the stuff that had accumulated. There were boxes that held not only his things and our sons' possessions, but also material from his parents, some dating back to their wedding in 1932. He wanted to experience the freedom he imagined would come with letting go, and he approached his task as a spiritual practice.

As he went through the boxes, he came across old personal letters, photographs of loved ones (as well as pictures of people he didn't know), citations for achievement, and mementos of all sorts. He debated what to let go of and what to hold on to. He had to ask himself what was the motivation for holding on. When he asked a friend how she decided, she told him she kept only the things that were of interest to her today. If they had been important in times past, she honored the memories and let the objects go.

There are no easy answers as we attempt to clear our clutter, make room, or simplify our lives, although all sorts of advice may be offered. Guidelines might help with the task, but if you are not willing to look at your motivations for holding on and letting go, cleaning becomes a chore rather than a spiritual practice. Author Phillip Harnden describes the practice this way: "We take delight in things; we take delight in being loosed from things. Between these two delights, we must dance our lives."[1]

INVITATION TO PRACTICE

Imagine a line with the delight of things at one end and the delight of being loosed from things at the other end. Where are you on this scale? Is that where you want to be? Are you willing to dance?

A Catholic friend explored this practice one year by deciding to give something away every day in Advent, the four weeks leading up to Christmas. The first days were easy as she got rid of things she realized she no longer wanted. She gave things to Goodwill, to friends, and a few things to the trash. But it got harder as she began to let go of things she loved. Through this practice she was reminded every day of her reasons for holding on or letting go.

Letting go of valued belongings is what makes the ancient Native American tradition of the "give-away" ceremony a spiritual practice. When people in these cultures are honored for birthdays, graduations, retirements, or other special occasions, they do not receive gifts from others, but rather they give cherished items to those who come to help them celebrate. "It is not the value of the gift, but the giving itself that is culturally relevant," writes Ray Buckley, who is Lakota/Tlingit. "Giving a gift that may not have significant monetary worth but significant spiritual or personal value is a sign of a giving heart."[2] The gifts received are not to be held on to but are given away at a later time. The rhythm is one of receiving, holding, and letting go.

INVITATION TO PRACTICE
What cherished possession might you be willing to give
away? What would it mean to you to do so?

Fasting: Making Space for the Sacred

Letting go as a spiritual practice is not just about releasing or giving away material possessions. Letting go is about making space, which can mean abstaining or not receiving. The ancient practice of fasting usually entails giving up food for a specific length of time for the purpose of cleansing body and soul and to make room for the Holy. In Islam, personal fasting throughout the year is encouraged to develop a deeper awareness of the divine Presence. In addition to periodic fasts, fasting during the month of Ramadan is obligatory for devout Muslims. They fast from sunup to sundown in appreciation and gratitude for the Qur'an, revealed to the Prophet Muhammad during this month fourteen hundred years ago.

Personal and public fasting are also part of the Jewish and Christian traditions. In addition to fasts for private reasons, Jews are called to fast on Yom Kippur, the Day of Atonement. The Hebrew scriptures contain this commandment: "This is to be a lasting ordinance for you: On the tenth day of the seventh month you must deny yourselves ... because on this day atonement will be made for you, to cleanse you. Then, before the Lord, you will be clean from all your sins" (Leviticus 16:29–31).

Early Christians were encouraged to fast on Wednesdays and Fridays, which in more modern times was reduced to abstaining from meat on Fridays. The forty days before Easter became the Christian period of penance for sins, known as Lent. Different churches and denominations suggest a variety of guidelines for this fast, but many Christians follow the general tradition of giving up some particular food for Lent.

In past years I have noticed a trend away from giving up food to giving up some other habit, such as the morning newspaper, sudoku puzzles, or romance novels. Some teenagers have reported giving up texting or posting on Facebook. A friend decided to give up gossip. Lent may be the catalyst for letting go of something, but giving up a harmful habit can happen any time.

In the middle of his second year of college, my younger stepson, Paul, announced that he was going to quit complaining. He told us he was tired of listening to his classmates grousing about homework, teachers, rules, food, and roommates. "You name it; they'll complain," he said. Then he added, "I realize I do the same thing. What a waste of time!" And he stopped. That was twelve years ago, and to this day he will say when he doesn't like something or speak up if something is wrong, but he really did let go of his habit of complaining.

Whether food or an activity or a way of behaving, the purpose for all fasting is to let go of something that guides our attention away from the divine Presence. By freeing our attention, we create an empty space in our lives. Since emptiness often feels unpleasant or even frightening, the temptation will be to quickly fill the space fasting has created. When I feel hungry from my food fast, can I sit with it and not try to distract myself with aimless activity? If the absence of my newspaper makes me feel restless in the morning, can I simply allow the anxiety and not fill the space with an electronic substitute? The challenge of fasting is to use the empty space and time for reflection, to become more self-aware, and to turn our attention to the sacredness of life. To make this more intentional, some people add an intentional feasting after their fast: "I will fast from gossip and feast on kindness," or "I will fast from discouragement and feast on encouragement."

INVITATION TO PRACTICE
What might you be willing to fast from to create space
and time for you to attend to the Holy?

Forgiveness: Letting Go of Hurts and Leaving the Past Behind

How often we are pulled from experiencing the holiness of the present moment by thoughts of our past. You might remember a particularly wonderful time in your life, wish it were like that again, and despair at all the difficulties now surrounding you. Maybe you had a hurtful encounter with a friend last week and are rehashing what was said, what you wished you'd said, and wondering how it might have turned out differently. You could be carrying a deeply disturbing memory you can't seem to let go of, and when it comes to mind, you go back over the incident again and again, retelling the story and rekindling old hurt and anger.

Wishing things were as they used to be, reworking old conversations, and telling our painful stories of abuse and injustice is natural.

But if we do so to place blame or dwell on another's guilt, our pain turns to resentment, and our lives fill with bitterness. Bitter people hold tightly to their past, remember every detail of the story, and sink into self-pity. Captured by past events, they are unable to move forward into new life. The possibility of forgiveness as a means of letting go of their hurt and bitterness may never have occurred to them.

Forgiveness keeps us from being stuck in the past and helps us find a way beyond the prison of bitterness. When we forgive, we let go of our emotional attachment to what has happened, but we do not forget or excuse the wrong that was done or the pain that was caused. Sometimes we are able to go to the person who has hurt us and offer them our forgiveness. Many more times forgiveness is something we do in our own hearts without engaging the other person face-to-face. Either way, forgiving another has no predictable outcome; it does not always lead to reconciliation, nor does it necessarily make a difference in the other person's life. What it can do is transform the person who has found the courage to forgive.

An emotionally abused woman went through the long complex process of forgiving her ex-husband. "Holding the anger and resentment was hurting me and my children," she said. "Through forgiveness I have been released. Although I remember with sadness what we all experienced, I have moved on with my life. Through forgiveness I have let him into my heart. I will never again let him into my house."

INVITATION TO PRACTICE
Is there someone in your life you need to forgive? Are you willing to explore ways to do that?

As you explore your ability to forgive others and seek the freedom that such willingness can bring, you will most likely become aware of some things you need to be forgiven for. When you recognize the hurt you have caused another, you may be able to write a letter or go to ask for forgiveness. But more often you will be faced with the hard task of forgiving yourself.

In my late thirties I let a dear friend down. She was counting on me, and I was not there for her. We did not speak of it, but we drifted apart. A few years later I learned she had died. I wept, wishing I had reached out to her, asking for forgiveness when she was alive. With her death, I felt there was no way to let go of the heaviness of heart that came from my betrayal. Over the ensuing years I have had to learn how to forgive myself. It has taken a long time. What I realized was that forgiving myself was not achieved through effort or willful action. Rather, forgiveness came through surrender—surrender to the reality of what I had done. I had to let go of my excuses, the rational reasons for my behavior, and my anger at her for her part in the friendship's end. When I was able to fully accept my guilt, I no longer needed to remain guilty. I was able to surrender into the arms of forgiveness.

The practice of letting go of past hurts, resentment, and bitterness may begin when we realize we have been holding on to something and turn to the process of forgiveness to set us free. As courageous as it is to forgive another or to forgive ourselves, the real challenge is to lead a forgiving and forgiven life. Rather than only attending to the large injustice or grievous hurt, are we willing to forgive the little mistakes and injuries that occur in everyday life? When another driver pulls into the parking space you were waiting for, can you nod pleasantly and move on? When the neighbor's child picks your spring tulips and comes to say she is sorry, can you forgive her? If you speak unkindly of someone and then recognize how unnecessary your words were, can you ask forgiveness for your thoughtlessness?

There are an infinite number of opportunities every day to hold on to little annoyances, to let the words or actions of another lodge in our hearts to fester and to be brought out later for study, examination, and complaint. When we do this, we need the reminder from this vivid piece of Hasidic wisdom: "Rake the muck this way. Rake the muck that way. It will still be muck. In the time you are brooding, you could be stringing pearls for the delight of heaven."[3]

Nonattachment: Letting Go of the Outcome

We are often attached to many things besides possessions, patterns of behavior, or old hurts. We may hang on to ideas, beliefs, traditions, or plans. And most likely we are very attached to the outcome of our endeavors—both large and small. When I prepare dinner for friends, I want the fish to be grilled just right, the green beans not overdone, and the rice cooked and seasoned to perfection.

Dedicated teachers want their students to learn and grow and flourish. Gardeners want the flowers to bloom. Doctors want their patients to get well. Activists working for justice and peace want to make the world a better place. We all want to be successful. But if we become attached to the outcome of our efforts, we may stumble in the process of moving forward. I could spoil my dinner party with my anxiety about perfection. In their desire to cure, doctors can lose sight of what their patients need. Attached to bringing about a peaceful world, activists may use less than peaceful means to bring about their goal. Writings and leaders from many religious traditions warn against this happening.

In the Bhagavad Gita, a sacred text of Hinduism, we find these words: "Do your duty, always; but without attachment. This is how one reaches the ultimate Truth; by working without anxiety about results."[4] When I read this passage aloud on a clergy renewal retreat, the pastors surprised me by hooting and breaking into spontaneous exclamations and conversation. After they calmed down, one of the participants announced that the previous evening they had been told by the hierarchy that they were to keep an exact count of the number of people attending worship every Sunday for the next six months. They knew that the success of their ministries would be judged by these specific results, the number of people filling their pews.

"You are suggesting a practice that goes against what we were told last night," one participant said. "I wonder what it would be like to simply preach the Gospel, build community, and serve the poor with our eyes on God and the people before us rather than on the results of our actions." "I know I would feel much less anxious," a seasoned pastor responded. "And I believe my ministry would flourish as a result."

A flourishing ministry might not be successful in the way this institution was measuring results, but Mother Teresa of Calcutta reminds us that God calls us to be faithful, not successful. And Jewish theologian Martin Buber was known to say that "success" is not a name of God. How do we practice letting go of the results of our labor in a culture that seems to worship success?

INVITATION TO PRACTICE

Have you ever entered into a project, a task, or an endeavor
with no attachment to an outcome? What was that like?

I have struggled with these teachings about attachment because I believed that if I were not attached, I would of necessity become detached. Detachment was to me synonymous with not caring. How could I not care about my writing, my teaching, my family? I didn't want to become withdrawn and passive, always on the margins of life. I wanted to be fully engaged. I realized I needed another place to stand and began to wonder what life might be like if I practiced *nonattachment* rather than detachment.

Although those words are similar, I experience them very differently. Whereas attachment and detachment are static positions in opposition to each other, nonattachment is a dynamic middle way. Although it rests between the two poles, it is not a place but rather a movement or energy. Nonattachment becomes the dance between attachment and detachment during which we can receive the gifts and avoid the dangers of each.

Attachment brings the gifts of engagement, passion, and risk. When I am writing a lecture, I am deeply attached to the ideas, to my desire to be clear and evocative and connected to the group that will hear my presentation. This engagement connects me with the material and the audience, gives passion to my words and delivery, and allows me to take risks in what I say and the stories I choose to tell. But if I become attached to having my words applauded, my ideas accepted, my lecture a huge success, I have succumbed to the dangers of attachment—enmeshment, self-deception, and the loss of vision. When I become aware of the dangers of attachment, I can counter my desire for success by moving toward the gifts of the opposite pole—detachment.

Detachment holds the gifts of perspective, clarity, and self-reflection. If, for example, you choose to serve abused women in the local safe house, you will need these gifts. You will need to stand back and see clearly what the women are coping with and the reality of their situations. You will need to hear the stories of the women and their feelings without drowning in them. You will need to reflect on your own life and choices if you wish to understand the lives and choices of others. But if you become too detached, you will experience the dangers of this extreme position and find yourself isolated, lacking compassion, and avoiding responsibility. Noticing when this begins to happen, you can move back toward the gifts of attachment and find new ways to reengage with the women you serve.

To live with an attitude of nonattachment is to dance your way between attachment and detachment. It is a process and a practice. You pay attention to where you are, to what is happening in your heart and mind; you notice if you are moving to one extreme or the other, then gently correct yourself toward the center. You gratefully accept the gifts from both sides of the polarity and dance away from the dangers. You are learning the dance of letting go and staying engaged. In the words of wisdom from the Sufi tradition, you are learning to "trust in God and tie your camel."

INVITATION TO PRACTICE

Another opportunity to dance between two polarities!
Is there a place in your life right now where you might
practice letting go and staying engaged?

Accepting the Life That Awaits Us

As we learn to live a life of nonattachment, the ultimate challenge is to let go of our future, the life we have planned. Think back to when you were a teenager or young adult and your life stretched before you. Most likely you had ideas of where you were heading and held pictures in your heart of what your life would be like. Maybe you imagined a life of adventure or marriage and a family. You might have had a certain job or career in mind—the military, medicine, teaching, or construction. You may have made plans to make your dreams come true, such as more education or ways to find the perfect mate. You probably began to follow these plans in pursuit of your dreams. Are you now living the life you planned?

When I ask this question of adults in the second half of life, the answer is almost always "no." Some are deeply disappointed that their lives didn't turn out as planned, and others rejoice in the life they are living. As one woman said with glee, "I couldn't have imagined this life, let alone planned it. It is pure gift!"

Rejoicing in the life you have does not mean that there has not been pain and loss. Death, divorce, illness, job loss, bankruptcy, and accidents often interrupt our plans and cause our dreams to die. However, pleasant surprises can also cause a change in plans if we are willing to entertain them—such as an invitation to travel, a proposal of marriage, or a job offer outside your chosen career. How do the losses and surprises that are common in all our lives lead some to deep disappointment and others to lives more fully lived?

The answer is not to stop planning. There is nothing inherently wrong with setting goals and making lists of how to proceed. The problem comes when we become attached to our plans and get upset, angry, or depressed when the plans don't work out. I like to plan as much as the next person, maybe more. I love planning trips—airline schedules, what to take, where to eat. As I finish reading one book, I plan what to read next. I enjoy planning celebrations for my family and friends and I am an inveterate list maker. I have been learning to hold these plans lightly and have discovered that the easier I am with the small disappointments, the more prepared I will be for the next inevitable major interruption. So I practice letting go in ordinary situations.

When the book I had planned to read is not available, can I let go and find another or go without a book for a while? When the family celebration must be cancelled due to illness, can I simply be sad and let it go? When the route I planned to travel is closed by construction, can I let go of my irritation and find another way? Might I even discover that these changes in plans hold new possibilities? Life becomes full and exciting when we learn the rhythm of planning and letting go.

INVITATION TO PRACTICE
How do you respond when your plans are stymied?
If you pay attention, I imagine you will have a chance to
answer that question today!

Even when people's lives are tragically interrupted and plans are turned upside down, it seems that the ability to move on is grounded in a willingness to let go of what was and embrace what is and what will be. In the most difficult situations, such as the birth of a special-needs child, the sudden early death of a spouse, or the collapse of a business, some people are able to let go—not without profound grief and disappointment, but with grace and trust in what will follow.

A friend told me of her nephew who at the age of forty-five is retiring from the navy. "How exciting," I responded. "The whole second half of life before him!" "He's not seeing it that way," she said. "From his college days of ROTC, his commission, and further education, he's had his heart set on regular promotions so that some day he would retire as an admiral. He was passed over the last time, and in the military at his age it is either 'up or out.'"

Everything in this man's life has gone according to plan. And now he is faced with a major loss. He will not have the life he imagined. Will he sink into despair and depression, or find the courage to see this as an opportunity to take his life in a new direction? I wonder if the key to which way he will go will be his ability to trust—trust in a reality that is unfolding toward healing and wholeness.

If we look back over our lives to those moments in time when our careful plans were mangled by circumstances, we may see the new possibilities that have grown from them. When a friend of mine was fired from her prestigious job, she felt her life was over. Her self-esteem plummeted, she wondered how she would support herself, and her natural hopefulness turned to despair. She sought help, knowing she could not travel this journey alone. She began to recognize the need for patience and the uselessness of urgent striving. She remembered the times in her life and the lives of family and friends when the greatest loss contained a gift. Time passed (not as quickly as she would have liked), new opportunities presented themselves, and with new confidence her hope was restored. Five years later she feels she is now living the life that was waiting for her.

INVITATION TO PRACTICE

When faced with the need to let go of your life plan,
how have you responded? What have you learned?

Trust and surrender seem to be at the heart of the spiritual practice of letting go. The paradox is that we cannot experience trust or surrender unless we are willing to let go in the small everyday experiences and in the larger, more life-shattering events. As much as we would like to practice trust first and plan for periods of surrender, the process does not work in that linear fashion. We must learn by letting go. Remember the trapeze artist high above us in the circus tent? Can we follow her example, swinging until we are ready, and then let loose our grip, trusting we will be caught?

How Are You Called to Practice?

As you participated in the invitations to practice embedded in the text, you may have realized that some of the practices could warrant further exploration. The idea is not to involve yourself in every practice, but to pay attention to what is your next step in the practice of letting go.

Although the trapeze artist lets go of everything at once, that is not the way in most of our ordinary lives. In fact, it is probably wise to proceed gradually, letting go of our grip gently, softly. Where do you need to begin? Letting go of your stuff? Fasting from habits and behaviors to create empty space in which the spirit can move?

At the heart of this practice, as in every other practice, is the willingness to pay attention to your inner and outer worlds. If you do not pay attention, you will continue to hold on to what you have always held close. You may recognize how this practice of letting go is connected to previously encouraged practices: ceasing frantic activity to rest, letting go of words to be silent, stopping effort and striving in meditation, or turning away from companionship for periods of solitude.

Is it important for you to look to your past and begin or continue the practice of forgiveness? Where and how would it be wise to start? Only you can know. How attached are you to the life you have planned, making you unable to see the life that may be waiting for you? Spend some time looking back and then forward. Courage is necessary to look at these issues, to accept what you see, and then to transform old patterns of holding on to a new willingness to let go. To remind yourself of the power of letting go, practice tightening your fists and gently opening your fingers wide, closing and opening, closing and opening. Do this anywhere and anytime. The wisdom of your body will guide you to the next step in the practice of letting go, freeing you for a life not yet imagined.

GUIDELINES FOR MORE EXTENDED PRACTICE

THE COURAGE TO FORGIVE

For this practice, I suggest you choose someone you wish to forgive for some small mistake or unintentional rudeness. In this way you can begin to become familiar with the process of forgiveness and start to develop a forgiving heart before you engage a person who has caused greater harm. You may wish to have writing materials with you.

- Find a place where you can sit quietly alone and not be interrupted. If possible, you might place an empty chair in front of you.

- Take a deep breath to settle yourself. Notice what you are feeling and thinking. Notice any bodily sensations.

- When you are ready, imagine the person you wish to forgive sitting across from you. Pay attention to what he or she looks like—body posture, clothing, and facial expression. Notice how you feel as you gaze at this person.

- Now imagine the words you wish to say. You may do that silently, speak them aloud, or write them down. Don't try to "do this right." Speak from your heart.

- Notice the effect your words have on the person opposite you. How does this make you feel? Might you wish to say more?

→ You may wish to end the practice here. However, you might want to hear what the other person has to say. If so, listen for his or her response.

→ This practice may turn into a dialogue, but only allow it to continue as long as it is helpful. Remember, you are in charge of this event.

→ When you feel complete with this session, let the image of the other fade from the chair, and turn your attention back to your own body—your feet on the floor and the chair supporting you. Pay attention to what you are feeling and thinking.

→ You may wish to end with writing what you have experienced and possibly a simple prayer of gratefulness for what you have learned about forgiveness.

DANCING NONATTACHMENT

→ Find a place where you can stand comfortably with enough space around you to move a step to either side. (If you prefer, you can do this activity seated.)

→ Feel your feet on the floor, unlock your knees, and center yourself with your breath.

→ When you are ready, take one step to the side (if seated, move your hands from center to one side). In this new place, allow your hands and your body to reflect your experience of attachment, using as much of your body as you are able.

→ As you find a position that feels true to your experience of attachment, experience it fully. Notice what feelings and thoughts go with this position. Stay here as long as you wish.

→ Taking a deep breath, let the position go, and move back to center. Take a moment to reflect on the experience of attachment, the movement, the letting go.

→ When you are ready, take one step to the other side, or move your hands in that direction. In this new place, allow your body to reflect your experience of detachment, using as much of your body as you are able.

- As you find a position that feels true to your experience of detachment, experience it fully. Notice what feelings and thoughts go with this position. Stay here as long as you wish.

- Taking a deep breath, let the position go, and move back to center.

- Take a moment to reflect on the experience of detachment, the movement, the letting go.

- Now the invitation is to create your own dance between attachment and detachment. Move at your own speed from one polarity to the other. While taking the position of attachment, recognize the gifts inherent in that place. As you also remember the dangers, move gently toward detachment. Find the gifts of detachment, then recognize the dangers and dance back toward the opposite experience.

- Allow your body to lead you as you dance your way between the two, discovering the dynamic place of nonattachment. Remember that nonattachment is not a set place; it is not static but filled with energy. Remember how frozen you may have felt in both attachment and detachment. Can you feel the energetic difference in nonattachment? The possibilities? The freedom?

- Continue the movement as long as it is helpful. When you have learned what you need, allow your body and your hands to come to rest. Pay attention to your body, feelings, and thoughts.

- You may wish to use your breath to offer a prayer of gratefulness for what your body has taught you.

6

THE
PRACTICE
of COMMUNITY

Discovering Support, Encouragement, and Interdependence

I am because we are, and because we are, therefore I am.

East African proverb

A number of years ago I stopped going to church regularly. Without clearly making a choice not to attend worship, I simply slipped away. I would find something else of interest to do on Sunday morning. I would become engrossed in the Sunday paper and the time to leave for church would slide past. On snowy days, it was easy to use the bad weather as an excuse to stay home, even though my church was less than a mile away! When I did attend, I left feeling empty, which gave me the perfect reason not to return.

This pattern of absenting myself from church had gone on for almost a year when I began to experience a subtle but growing desire to be with others in worship. I was feeling alone on my spiritual journey and was at risk of becoming isolated. I needed to experience surrendering my individuality to something larger. I realized I was longing for a spiritual community. As an introvert, I usually avoid being in groups, so this desire to worship with others seemed odd. Then I remembered a classmate in seminary saying to me as I was resisting joining a church, "You can't be a Christian alone, Jane."

INVITATION TO PRACTICE

Try that phrase on for yourself. Select your own word
and use your own name: "You can't be a _____
alone, _____."

The importance of community is inherent in other religious traditions as well as in Christianity. Buddhist practitioners are taught to take refuge in the Three Jewels—the Buddha, the dharma, and the *sangha*. The Buddha is the awakened one, whose awakening all Buddhists aspire to. The dharma is the collection of the Buddha's teachings, and the *sangha* is the community comprising all those who honor the wisdom of the Buddha's teachings and who wish to end suffering.[1]

In the Jewish tradition, public prayer and other public religious obligations require a *minyan*, the word in Hebrew that means "to count," and in Orthodox Judaism refers to a quorum of ten Jewish men. In non-Orthodox congregations, the male requirement has been dropped, and adult women can be counted in the minyan.[2]

Community is necessary for many nonreligious spiritual practices as well. You can't be in a 12-step recovery program alone. You can't run in a relay race without your teammates. You need a partner to dance the tango. When we engage spiritual practices in community, we become part of something larger in which we are necessary, but where everything does not depend on us. "Humans are inseparable from community, just as planets are from galaxies," writes Cynthia Winton-Henry, co-founder of InterPlay. "We know our connection acutely, recognizing how much we need the company we keep."[3]

The Rhythm of Contemplative, Communal, and Missional Spiritual Practices

As I was struggling with my longing for church, I remembered the idea that all spiritual practices can be divided into three categories: contemplative practices, communal practices, and missional practices. Although we will never achieve a perfect balance of the three, we can find a rhythm that allows us to move gracefully among them, touching each category in our life of practice. I realized that my spiritual practices were either contemplative (caring for my body, resting, being silent, practicing solitude, and letting go) or missional (hospitality and service, which included my ministry of teaching, spiritual direction, and writing). Except for monthly spiritual direction and a monthly contemplative spiritual direction peer supervision group, I was practicing alone. I was way out of balance. I tentatively began attending church and now have returned full-time. I am finding once again the joy of participating in a diverse community where we gather together to share our progressive faith.

INVITATION TO PRACTICE

What are your communal spiritual practices? Look beyond your church, mosque, or synagogue to 12-step meetings, book clubs, prayer groups, or any other way you gather with others to pay attention to the holy in your life.

As you reflect on the rhythm of spiritual practices in your life, you may realize that the demarcation between solitary, communal, and missional practices is not neat and tidy. In our exploration of the practice of silence, we noticed the difference between being silent alone and honoring silence in community. In the practice of hospitality, we will explore the contemplative practice of welcoming our inner strangers, in addition to the missional practice of offering hospitality to others. Although we can engage the practice of service on our own, we will recognize how often we need a community to reach out to others. Since all our practices interconnect with each other, it may be hard to find balance or to determine just how much time we spend in one category or another.

Because of this difficulty of finding balance, I prefer to seek a rhythm among the different practices. Balance implies an equal division, whereas rhythm gives a sense of graceful movement and flow. Depending on the stage of life we are in and our personalities, we will be drawn more to one category or another. As an introvert, I easily attend to contemplative practices. My extroverted friends spend much more time in communal and missional practices. Young parents often tell me they have little opportunity for solitude or silence, whereas the homebound often long for the opportunity to be with a group. I believe that your rhythm will be shaped by who you are and your life situation. Over the years it will shift and change as your life unfolds. There is no right or wrong way to move among the three categories. Your awareness of them can help you include at least a taste of all three. Listen to your soul. By its longing you will know where to focus your attention.

INVITATION TO PRACTICE

What is the contemplative versus communal rhythm in your life right now? Are you aware of any soul stirrings that might guide you to a different rhythm?

In the following pages, as we explore a number of communal practices, pay attention to your existing rhythm as well as the desires of your soul. Let the stories and ideas help you become aware of practices that you may be ignoring, as well as the communal practices you are already involved in. Let your mind and heart open to new possibilities, even as you affirm your existing pattern of practice.

Singing Together We Become the Music

In chapter 1, I wrote about the man who remembered being surrounded by the singing of his extended family and claimed that experience as an early spiritual gift. His experience is one I have never had. Music was not part of my family of origin. We neither made music nor listened to music. We talked, we read, and we played games together, but music was absent. As a result, I have resisted any invitation to sing. I attended a workshop once where the leader asked us to stand in a circle and sing our names. I fled.

I knew I was missing something by silencing my singing voice. Throughout history people have found spiritual sustenance in song. Hildegard of Bingen, twelfth-century mystic and musician, believed the human voice was created for praising the Divine Mystery. She wrote, "The body is the garment of the soul and it is the soul which gives life to the voice. That's why the body must raise its voice in harmony with the soul for the praise of God."[4]

Although I am not planning to take singing lessons, I am trying to overcome my hesitancy to sing out. When alone, I practice humming or singing a familiar phrase from a nursery rhyme or an old popular tune. I play with simply giving voice to a variety of tones, creating my own song without words. I feel the vibrations resonate in my chest and belly, and I understand the old saying that "those who sing, pray twice."

INVITATION TO PRACTICE
Are you willing, at any odd moment, to break into song,
or chant, or tone? Try it!

I think one aspect of my desire to return to community worship was the opportunity to sing—to join my voice with others in praise and commitment. This longing was clarified for me one day when I attended a fundraising luncheon. The keynote speaker was

Dr. Arthur Jones, founder of the Spirituals Project, an organization dedicated to educating communities about the powerful tradition of African American spirituals. Dr. Jones spoke briefly about the healing power of song and then invited an unsuspecting audience to join their voices with his to feel what happens when we sing in community.

There was a flutter of nervousness in the room as he began to sing, "Sometimes I feel like a motherless child, a long way from home." Hesitantly we joined him, following his lead, repeating the verses, until the room swelled with connection and emotion. We were inside the music. We had become the music.

As our voices subsided, we sat for a moment savoring the experience. Then Dr. Jones gave words to what had happened. He spoke about how all of us know the truth of the words of the song. We have all felt abandoned and alone. We know the grief and the sadness of a motherless child. By singing together, we discovered that we are not alone in our grief and that we can be soothed by the connections to one another. "You discover you can survive and thrive," he said, "and make the world a better place."[5]

INVITATION TO PRACTICE
Find a place where you can sing or chant with others.
Rather than worrying about how you sound, focus your
attention on becoming the music.

Singing together can be full of celebration and joy, as well as a time of recollection. A Jewish friend of mine told me that the primary reason she goes to synagogue is to participate in the music. "I love to sing the old songs in Hebrew," she said. "I don't need to know the meaning of the words. The music that has been part of our tradition forever resonates in my body, and I feel connected to all those present and all who have gone before."

When the songs we share are joyful, our feelings are enhanced by the blessed community. When they are mournful, the connections with others may help us discover hope and realize the possibility that we can survive and thrive together.

Dancing, Moving, and Playing Together

In the same way that singing draws on our collective energies to inspire, heal, and energize, movement expresses our communal joy as we dance at weddings and other celebrations. If we allow our bodies to express our grief as well as our joy, our pain may ease when our feelings are held by a wider community.

Before my mother's death in 1993, I had begun moving and dancing with a group of women one morning a week. We had come together with the desire for an embodied spiritual practice, to move from the inside out, and to discover what our bodies had to teach us. We engaged in little conversation. Our leader, Chris, gathered us together, helped us stretch and warm up, and then offered us a little guidance—usually in the form of questions. She provided evocative music, and we lived her motto: "Show up, shut up, and dance."

My mother's memorial service in the town in California where I grew up had been beautiful and sweet. The church was full (which she would have liked), the flowers abundant, and the music rich and vibrant. The minister gave a moving summary of her life, and those chosen to speak gave tribute to her generosity, her compassion, and her listening heart. We were all well dressed and well behaved. No one cried, and I found myself longing for another way to express my grief.

In the first class after returning home to Denver, Chris asked me if it would be helpful to dance my grief. "Not alone!" I exclaimed. "Oh no," she said. "We will all dance with you."

What followed was exactly what I needed. Chris invited the group to move in ways that would honor my grief, while at the same time connecting to their own. As the music started each woman began to move in her own space. I felt the permission and encouragement as I began to twist and spiral, descend to the floor, and rise again. Slowly we added sound to support our dance. Without planning or direction, our individual movements and voices intertwined, and we became one in the expression of grief. The sadness, too much for my small body, was being held and expressed by the body of this loving tribe.

INVITATION TO PRACTICE

When has your joy been recognized or your struggles accepted by an embodied community? How can that experience as a spiritual practice be sought out more intentionally?

Soon after this profound experience, Chris stopped teaching, and I was left without a tribe to dance with. I missed the embodiment of my spiritual practice and the movement community that had formed. In its absence, I turned my attention to other forms of spiritual practice, but nothing quite nurtured my soul in the same way dancing did. Then I discovered Cynthia Winton-Henry's book: *Dance—The Sacred Art: The Joy of Movement as a Spiritual Practice.* Winton-Henry is the cofounder of InterPlay. I knew that with this book she was not just encouraging us to dance as a spiritual practice, she was inviting us to enter into all movement with a sense of play. As I read her book, I could feel the longing in my body to move once again in community, but I hesitated. I was willing to dance, but could I overcome my aversion to play?

Play invites us to be spontaneous, silly, and free. We make fools of ourselves and don't care. We don't worry what we look or sound like. We laugh with abandon. Play has no goal except to joyfully engage others and the world. Although play is an integral part of childhood, it is not natural for most adults, who often harbor feelings of self-consciousness and the sense of preserving carefully crafted and controlled appearances. As adults, we often come to believe that foolishness is a waste of time and that we need to attend to the serious things of life.

I was an obedient, serious child. I followed rules; I got good grades. I learned to play games that required skill; I became competitive, and I loved to win. This pattern continued into my adult years. I was not a playful person. And I knew from reading Winton-Henry's book that if I wanted to dance, I would have to learn to play. I decided to risk it!

INVITATION TO PRACTICE
What is your history of play? In what ways are you playful? When and where do you resist play?

I found a local InterPlay group and I have (mostly) lost my inhibitions. We stretch and move—walking, running, stopping. We roar at each other like lions and pull back into turtle shapes. We throw imaginary paint balls around the room and practice fake Tai Chi. Working in pairs, we babble about nonsensical things. We join hands and create hand dances that have never been danced before. Throughout our time together we are invited to notice what is going on in our bodies, feelings, and minds. We end our *playshops* (as opposed to *workshops!*) in a circle, creating a song of tones, words, and rhythms, blending our voices in an expression of farewell. I leave renewed, refreshed, and grateful. I am back in touch with my body, and I have had fun! I could not have had this playful experience alone. It took a community to teach me to play.

Making Music Together: Surrendering to the Whole

All of us have a voice to share if we are willing to find a group for singing. We all have bodies that move, and we can discover new awareness and joy when we dance and play together. But not all of us play a musical instrument. Those of you who do have most likely spent years alone with your instrument, and you recognize that time to be a solitary spiritual practice. I have heard musicians talk about the joy that comes as they master a difficult piece on their flute, violin, or piano. But most of them are quick to say that their singular practice is in the service of bringing their gifts to a larger whole, whether it is a jazz ensemble, a band, a drumming circle, a string quartet, or a full orchestra.

Instrumental music becomes a communal spiritual practice when people make music together, finding their way to blend tones and rhythms to create what none of them could produce alone. The wonder of this accomplishment becomes a spiritual practice, not only for those who make the music, but also for the rest of us who listen with open hearts.

One person who cannot practice her art alone, who depends on a community from the very beginning, is the orchestra conductor. Marin Alsop, former conductor of the Colorado Symphony, tells about the difficulty she had when she realized she wanted to become a conductor. "Unlike my friends who could go into their rooms to practice their instruments," she said, "I needed a group to practice! There is no way you can learn to conduct on your own." I believe her words are true for us in many areas of our own lives. We cannot awaken and become fully alive by ourselves. We need each other; we need to learn how to surrender our individual gifts for the benefit of the whole.

Some music is created by groups with no established conductor or leader. In jazz improvisation, the creative process calls the musicians to listen to each other, blending their instruments, sometimes following and other times taking the lead. This interdependence is what we learn when we engage in spiritual practice in community. We learn to intuit when we are to lead and when we are to follow. Practicing together, we are more able to hear the call to surrender to the leading of the spirit, letting go of our own agenda to become one with the whole.

Jenny is a professional drummer who echoes this experience when she participates in spontaneous drumming circles. "My drum adds to the whole," she said. "I become part of something bigger, then I become one with it, and ultimately something even bigger is born." She also shared another reason why drumming with others is a spiritual practice for her. "I learn a lot about myself when I play with strangers," she told me. "I might make judgments about a person as we begin to play. Then something happens—maybe a beautiful new rhythm, a subtle transition, a graceful shift from leading to following—and I am forced to change my perceptions of another. By recognizing my own prejudices, I can let them go and see that other person anew."

If you do not play a musical instrument, you are not shut out of experiencing music as a spiritual practice. You can participate by listening, by attending to unique sounds as well as the whole, by feeling when a group seems to transcend the skills of the individuals and creates a magnificent new thing. Listen to the music with your whole body, feeling the rhythms and tones in your organs and bones. Allow the music to touch your emotions. Simply notice and feel what is evoked without trying to figure anything out. With this attentiveness you will be able to experience music as a spiritual practice.

A friend who was visiting a small town on the west coast of Florida stumbled across a Saturday night ritual on the local beach. For years people have been gathering there to drum the sun down. "There was no leader," she told me. "The drummers simply gathered around each other. Everyone was welcomed. There was no program, no seeming order, and very few words. The setting sun was directing the music. Children played in the open spaces, and sometimes a few people danced. Hundreds came every week, joining together in celebration of the rhythms of life."

INVITATION TO PRACTICE

In the next month find somewhere to go where others are making music. Allow their gifts to help you feel fully alive.

Spiritual Direction

Singing, dancing, and making music are only a few of many possible communal spiritual practices. Storytelling is practiced in many communities to keep alive and pass on important spiritual traditions. Community gardening is another spiritual practice where land and equipment, knowledge and skills, are shared to bring forth a bounty no one person could produce alone. I'm sure you can think of many more. Look to those places in your life when people come together to work or play, study or pray, and where everyone is valued for their unique gifts and the sum is always greater than the parts.

Another quite different form of communal practice, which often consists of just two people, is spiritual direction. I first encountered spiritual direction years ago during my first year in seminary. I took a class on the history of Christian spirituality taught by a Catholic priest at the Jesuit School. I was among the few Protestants present. In the course of one lecture the priest mentioned something called spiritual direction. I think he assumed everyone knew what that was, so he didn't elaborate. But I was intrigued. Could it be there was someone who could help me attend to my spiritual life in this highly academic and competitive environment? Might there be someone willing to listen to my heart?

After class I introduced myself to the professor and asked whether I needed to be Catholic to have a spiritual director. He smiled. "No," he said. "Do you want one?" He gave me the name of a woman near the school, and I called her the next day. She asked when I wanted to meet. I told her as soon as possible. We made the first appointment in what was to be a six-year relationship that became a deep blessing in my life.

The formal practice of spiritual direction began in medieval times when young men and women were joining monasteries and convents and were in need of spiritual guidance to grow into mature monks and nuns. The ancient tradition assumed the spiritual director to be superior to the person receiving direction. The director had all the wisdom the young person needed and proceeded to impart that knowledge and wisdom from a place of authority. The directee's role was simply to receive and be formed by the director.

Over the centuries the tradition of spiritual direction has continued but has seen many changes. Today, director and directee are more often understood to be equals, but having different roles. The image I use is of the two walking a path together. The director holds the lamp so they can see where they are going. She may shine the light in different ways and in different directions and invite the directee to explore what he sees. In earlier times, the director spoke and the directee listened. This has been reversed, so today the directee does most of the talking, while the director listens with an open heart and may ask gentle question to invite deeper reflection.

INVITATION TO PRACTICE
If this description of the practice of spiritual direction touches a place of longing within you, what do you want to do with that longing?

Spiritual direction is not religious training and is no longer the exclusive practice for the formation of nuns and monks. It has grown beyond the monasteries and is available to those of any faith tradition or of no belief system. Although the practice has Christian roots, a Buddhist student who entered my class believing she had no idea what spiritual direction was, later said as we explored and experienced spiritual direction together, that she realized it was much like the spiritual relationship she had with her teacher. The professional organization, Spiritual Directors International, expresses how inclusive spiritual direction has become in their guiding statement: "Tending the Holy around the world and across traditions."[6] Because of these changes, some people prefer to describe the practice as "spiritual guidance," "spiritual friendship," or "soul friending."

I have included the practice of spiritual direction in this chapter on communal practices because of its interactional nature, but it fits with the contemplative and missional practices as well. Spiritual direction is contemplative, for it helps us listen for the still, small voice of the spirit. Sitting with another listening heart helps us pay attention to our lives. When the director holds the lamp high, we may be able to see our lives in a new way. His or her caring presence may give us courage to feel our grief, live in our desert places, or discover new joys. My director helps me embrace the mystery and wonder of my life.

For twenty-five years I have been offering spiritual direction, and I experience sitting with another as a missional practice. I am practicing hospitality by providing a beautiful and safe place for the person who comes. I offer an open, hospitable heart, receiving his grief and joy; her fears, doubts, and disappointments. Every aspect of a person's life is welcome in spiritual direction. Just as those who come to me, I too need the same hospitality for my own soul. Although I have had to change directors a few times over the years, I have not stopped receiving direction. I cannot imagine doing the ministry I do without the loving companionship of a director.

How Are You Called to Practice?

There are many more communal spiritual practices than the ones explored in this chapter—attending worship, making music, moving playfully, and engaging in spiritual direction. You might be part of a knitting or sewing circle. Maybe you attend a monthly meditation group or a weekly photography class. Look to the groups you already belong to and see if you might name the activities as spiritual practices. They may not be part of a religious tradition, but if you leave the group feeling more awake and alive, you probably have been engaging in spiritual practice.

Maybe you are part of a religious tradition and have not been attending services. If that is so for you, don't ask yourself why. *Why* is not usually a helpful question, for it can take us into our heads and tends to make us defensive. Ask instead if there is anything at worship that you miss or anything there that could refresh your spirit. Think about choosing to attend or not based on the wisdom of your body and soul.

Do the stories of music and movement bring a longing to your heart? Or do you think, "That is the *last* thing I want to do"? Honor your initial response, but also notice if the thing you don't want to do is exactly what you may need to do. Sometimes the spirit moves us by providing us with a strong negative response. When it first occurred to me to go to seminary, everything inside of me shouted, "*No!*" I had to ask myself whether that intense response was because I knew, on some deep level, that's what I needed to do.

You may not want to engage in formal spiritual direction, but see if finding a spiritual friend might be an important practice for you. You may already have someone in your life you can talk to about issues of meaning and purpose, someone who listens well, helps you probe your questions deeply, and refrains from giving advice. Maybe you have noticed that people seek you out for these kinds of conversations. Could it be that you are already participating in informal spiritual direction?

Some of you may be aware that you are already engaged in many forms of communal practice. Maybe you don't need to add anything more. But you might take time to look closely at those activities you are involved with. Are they still nurturing your soul? Have they become deadening rather than enlivening? Are you doing them out of habit? Might it be time to let go of some of your communal activities?

The first extended practice is designed to help you see just where you are in relation to communal practices and what else, if anything, you may wish to do. The second practice is an invitation to play a simple game in which three volunteers create a sculpture with their bodies, leaving the rest of the group to creatively name what is seen.

GUIDELINES FOR MORE EXTENDED PRACTICE

MY COMMUNAL SPIRITUAL PRACTICE: EXAMINING ITS HISTORY AND DISCOVERING ITS FUTURE

You may wish to have paper and pencil for the early part of this practice. There will be a number of questions to reflect on, and instead of trying to remember earlier thoughts, I have found it helpful to make notes to myself.

> Find a place where you can sit comfortably and alert. Take a couple of deep breaths, allowing your body to relax and your mind and heart to open.

> Bring to mind communities of your early years. Were you part of a temple, synagogue, or church? Did you belong to clubs or organizations that had special creative activities such as drama, writing, music, or drawing? Were you involved with others in service projects? How did you feel about your practices within these communities? Did they nurture you?

> Move your attention to early adulthood, looking at the communities from that period. Ask yourself the same questions, looking for the places and people that refreshed your spirit. What groups and practices did you leave behind? How did you discover the new ones?

> Pay attention to your life right now. What are your communal practices? Are there any from earlier times of your life that you miss? How do the practices today relate to your past experiences? Has the focus of these groups changed? Has there been consistency in your communal practices in different stages of your life?

> Look over what you have written or remembered, and reflect on any patterns you see in your spiritual practices. Do not judge; simply notice.

⇒ Put your writing and your reflection aside. Take a few deep breaths, and turn your attention to the future. Which of your practices do you wish to continue? Are there any you would like to let go of? Are there new ones beckoning to you?

⇒ Complete this reflection when you are ready. You may be aware of some particular action you are being called to. You may not. See if you are able to allow whatever is present in your body, mind, and spirit, and trust that if there is something to be done, you will know in the future what it is.

PLAYFUL BODY SCULPTING AND CREATIVE NAMING

This simple and easy group activity can be done in any setting where a break is needed from sitting, thinking, and talking. It is easy to do and is designed to include those who simply wish to observe. You will need at least six people, but it could be done with a group of fifteen to twenty.

⇒ Gather in a circle with room in the middle for movement.

⇒ Give the group these simple instructions: "One person will take a body position in the center of the circle and remain still. Another person will join him or her, with their body shape connected to the first person. Then a third person will join the other two."

⇒ When the group sculpture is complete, those in the circle will gaze at it and see if they might name what they see. There is no right or wrong answer.

⇒ After the naming, the sculpture dissolves and the participants return to the circle.

⇒ The person who did the naming is the one to start again in the center of the circle, inviting two other volunteers to join, and the process is repeated.

⇒ The naming and dissolving of the sculpture allows for another and then another to be formed.

My experience is that the movement and the naming become more creative as people enter into the spirit of play. They return from this activity to the task at hand refreshed and renewed.[7]

7

THE
PRACTICE
OF HOSPITALITY

Inviting, Welcoming, and Nurturing the Stranger

Training in equanimity is learning to open the door to all,
welcoming all beings, inviting life to come visit.

Pema Chodron

"I have invited a young Japanese woman named Orie to live with us
for the summer," my older stepson Jamie wrote from Kyoto. "She
is the sister of a friend I met on my high school visit to Takayama.
She is coming to Denver to study English and needs a place to stay."
That letter was the beginning of a journey of hospitality that Jim and
I didn't initiate but did agree to.

As summer approached and Orie's arrival drew near, I was of two
minds. I was pleased with Jamie's attitude of hospitality, his recognition of another's need, and his desire to share from his abundance.
At the same time I knew how busy the summer was going to be, the
extra work a guest would entail, and the energy it would take for this
introvert to be welcoming and nurturing. I imagined she would need a
lot of care and attention while she was with us. We had never before

had a guest in our home for more than a week. I was stepping into a great unknown and was not sure I wanted this particular adventure. I felt like an obligation had been thrust upon me.

I began the preparations and attended to the details of her arrival with a sense of duty. I arranged her room and wrote a note of welcome to put with the flowers on the dresser. Jim contacted the University of Denver to find her class assignments and where those classes would take place. He studied the bus schedules so he could teach her how to get to school and back. Behind this preparation were so many questions and worries: How good was her English? Would we be able to communicate? Was she needy or independent? Might she cause trouble? Would we like her? What if she didn't like us?

The first few days of her visit were more chaotic than I had imagined. Everything needed to be negotiated—decisions about meals, unexpected needs, misunderstandings due to language, changed schedules, jet lag, and homesickness. Jim and I were both working. Jamie and his brother Paul had their own schedules. Where was I to find a moment of peace, space for quiet, or time for reflection? I woke up each morning overwhelmed by the thought of the coming day but determined to get through it as best I could. I wondered if I would survive the summer.

The next week, lying in bed early one morning, I became aware that I had opened our home to Orie, but I had not opened my heart. I realized I had a choice. I could duty through the next three months, or I could welcome each day with its surprises and unexpected gifts. The practice of hospitality might not get easier, but surely it could become much more fun.

The Three Movements of Hospitality

Religious traditions observe the practice of hospitality as a sacred call. In the Abrahamic religions, hospitality to others is founded on the divine hospitality that lies at the heart of creation—God having provided us with a home on earth (Genesis 1:1–31). When we welcome the stranger into our homes, worksites, neighborhoods, and places of worship, we model our actions on God's nurturing impulse. Beyond the gift of creation, the generous image of God as host is found in the Hebrew scriptures when God provides manna and daily quail to the Israelites wandering in the wilderness (Exodus 16:4–14).

Abraham becomes the first biblical model for human hospitality in the book of Genesis (18:1–10). When three strangers appear at Abraham's tent, he addresses them respectfully and invites them in, welcoming them with water to wash their feet and an opportunity to rest. With his wife, Sarah, and his servant, Abraham prepares a feast for the guests. The identity of the visitors as messengers from God is only revealed later when they tell Abraham and Sarah they will be blessed in their old age with a son. In the Christian scriptures, the writer of the letter to the Hebrews refers to this story when he writes, "Do not neglect to show hospitality to strangers, for thereby some have entertained angels unaware" (Hebrews 13:2).

Throughout the Gospels Jesus is described as a generous host, opening his heart and his table to all who came his way. He also gave clear instructions to the people as to whom should be invited to their banquets. His listeners are warned against inviting their friends and rich neighbors, who will likely repay them. Rather, he says to "invite the poor, the maimed, the lame, the blind, and you will be blessed, because they cannot repay you" (Luke 14:12–14).

This theme of inviting those who cannot reciprocate is continued in Islam. Muhammad was known for his generous hospitality. He welcomed into his home the rich and the poor, friend and foe, as well as those from other religious traditions. In the Qur'an we read, "They feed with food the needy wretch, the orphan, and the prisoner, for love of Him, saying, 'We wish for no reward nor thanks from you'" (76:8–9). The emphasis on welcoming and nurturing those who have no chance to repay seems to indicate that inclusive hospitality mirrors the radical hospitality of God.

INVITATION TO PRACTICE
Where do you experience the radical hospitality of God?

Radical hospitality is taught in other world religions as well. Fundamental to Hindu culture is the tradition that regardless of how poor one is, all strangers must be offered three expressions of welcome: sweet words, a sitting place, and refreshments (at least a glass of water).[1] This teaching is based on the oldest sacred texts of Hinduism: "The husband and wife of the house should not turn away any who comes at eating time and asks for food. If food is not available, a place to rest, water for refreshing one's self, a reed mat to lay one's self on, and pleasing words entertaining the guest—these at least never fail in the houses of the good" (Apastamba Dharma Sutra 8.2).

A similar message is found today in Native American cultures. From Winnebago precepts come these words: "See to it that whoever enters your house obtains something to eat, however little you may have. Such food will be a source of death to you if you withhold it."[2]

As evidenced in the stories told above, the world's major faith traditions indicate that the spiritual practice of hospitality has three basic movements: inviting, welcoming, and nurturing. The invitation can occur in a moment and could be offered by you or someone else. Your spouse might invite coworkers over for dinner before consulting you. Jamie issued the invitation to Orie on the spur of the moment.

Welcoming, the second movement of the practice of hospitality, can also be fairly simple and accomplished without too much time or energy. Guests are greeted at the door; a meal has been prepared, or a room made ready. Nurture, the third movement, can be much more challenging, because it involves sustaining hospitality.

In retrospect I can see that in my experience with Orie I was quite able to negotiate invitation and welcome, the first two movements of hospitality. Jamie had invited Orie, and we had welcomed her.

Nurture, the third movement, was proving much more difficult, for it called for a change of heart, presence as well as words. My morning realization was a turning point. I plunged into the depths of hospitality.

With my heart open, I discovered a brave young woman—eager to learn, hopeful and helpful, ready for new experiences. She loved accompanying us to church, to meetings, and to plays she could not understand. As her English improved, we could talk about more than the weather and the day's schedule, and I realized what a great leap of faith she had made in coming to Denver. As she felt more at home, she asked if she could bring some school friends for dinner, and some evenings we had several languages around our table. We discovered that she and I shared the same birthday, and on July 25 we went to a local Japanese restaurant to celebrate. Orie dressed in her finest kimono.

At the end of the summer we helped her find a tiny apartment on her own—a new adventure for her, one she might never have experienced in Japan. Even though she was no longer under our roof, we were still her Denver family and remain so twelve years later. After a few years we were able to visit her family in Takayama, then she visited again for two weeks on her way to another language school in New York. Last year she brought her new husband, Hiro, to meet us. She told me then how she treasured the note I had left for her the day she first arrived. "You wrote, 'Welcome to our home,'" she said. "I will never forget."[3]

INVITATION TO PRACTICE

When have you offered a stranger hospitality? What did you learn? Share your story with someone before the end of this week.

Hospitality: A Two-Way Street

I am aware that all stories of hospitality do not end as well as mine. I have heard of a guest invited for a week who left three months later; or the guest who, after a warm welcome, left with the family silver. Other hosts have told me about the difficulties of continued nurture when guests took much more time and energy than expected. One family had to struggle with a guest who did not abide by house rules; and another who set a bad example for their children. One woman told me how difficult it was when she and her husband had to ask a guest to leave after they realized the arrangement would not work. To their surprise, three years later they received a letter from the guest telling them how important their initial hospitality had been and apologizing for her part in the termination of the relationship. You may never know how a guest's heart has been touched or his or her life transformed from receiving your gift of hospitality. Much time may pass before you realize that the transformed life could be your own.

True hospitality is a two-way street. The possibility of transformation is present for all involved. Although there may be designated hosts and guests, there is a mutuality of gifts given and received. Although the guests usually have the obvious needs—food, a safe place, a personal connection—the hosts have needs as well. When I welcomed Orie into our home, I had no idea I needed to let go of control and allow family life to expand and deepen. As she received the gifts we offered—shelter, friendship, respect, admiration—we received her good humor, her spontaneity, and her feisty feminine presence in a predominantly male household. All were well served.

Along with the gifts, acts of hospitality also contain difficulties and struggles for both hosts and guests. All hospitality comes with a cost. For the hosts, the price is spending time and energy as well as money. For the guests, the cost is being dependent and likely experiencing a sense of being beholden. In the third movement of nurturing guests, boundaries may have to be negotiated, important life questions may rise for discussion, and confusion and conflict may need to be sorted out. A guest might be frightened and require constant reassurance. Another might be acting out and need clear boundaries and guidance on appropriate behavior. In addition, as relationships between hosts and guests deepen, all are called to more vulnerability, presence, and love. If you choose to practice hospitality, all aspects must be considered. Even then there will be surprises, disappointments, and unexpected gifts. Offering hospitality sets things in motion that we are not able to control.

Downtoward B + P

INVITATION TO PRACTICE

Is there someone, not necessarily a stranger, you might like to invite into your home? Maybe just for tea? Notice the state of your mind and heart as you practice inviting, welcoming, and nurturing your guest.

Practicing Communal Hospitality:
Blessings and Challenges

The spiritual practice of hospitality often begins at home and with our personal relationships. But expanding our personal practice of hospitality beyond the walls of our homes can have transformative effects on the community as a whole. Hospitality offered by a community—in temples, mosques, and churches, as well as in secular institutions such as schools, places of work, and community centers—has the advantage of combined resources as well as more hands and hearts to welcome and nurture those who come.

A small inner-city church in Denver offers a Saturday lunch program for persons with chronic mental illness. Guests begin arriving at ten o'clock when the doors open. Many of the participants know each other, and they gather early for the fellowship as well as the food. When new people arrive, they are welcomed by guests and volunteers alike. Round tables in the church basement are set with flowers, cutlery, butter, and salt and pepper. Coffee, tea, and juices are available, as well as fresh fruit and warm rolls.

Around eleven o'clock, lunch is served by the volunteers. The guests help themselves to salad, but the main course and a homemade dessert are served to them. Often there are special requests—"No green beans for me!" "Double on the potatoes, please!" "I'm saving room for dessert!" Over the meal, stories are told and resources shared. Often there are bursts of laughter, and occasionally tears are shed. When the meal is over, containers of leftovers are prepared, and the guests leave with shouts of "Good-bye!" "God bless you!" "Thank you!" and "See you next week."

This program has been in existence for over fifteen years and is able to sustain the three movements of hospitality because of the cooperation of three church communities that share one building. The different congregations take turns, volunteers come and go; but from September through May the guests know that they have been issued a sincere invitation, a warm welcome awaits them, and they will be nurtured by a hot meal and fellowship every Saturday.

Although this program has been successful over a long period of time, offering communal hospitality can run into difficulties. One group within the congregation may be excited about offering their basement for homeless women, and another group may oppose it for a variety of reasons. Sometimes an invitation is offered without thought of what welcome and nurture may entail. When a congregation issues an invitation by posting a sign saying, "EVERYONE IS WELCOME HERE," are they really willing to welcome and nurture everyone? What about the person who interrupts the sermon, talking back to the preacher? What of the family who arrives at worship not speaking the language of the congregation? Do we really want the person reeking of alcohol near the Sunday school? I have known churches that serve their communities with active food programs. People in need are received at the pantry, but these Saturday clients may not be welcome in Sunday worship.

A mainline church in a small city in the Midwest that prided itself on offering full hospitality to all found themselves in great conflict. Situated on the boundary between a solid middle-class neighborhood and an impoverished area, they were used to people from the margins of society participating in all aspects of congregational life. Those who came were not only offered food and fellowship, they were given a safe place to rest.

One man from the streets who had been coming regularly suddenly began to exhibit angry behavior. He would enter into arguments about any and everything. His voice would rise, and his angry gestures would become more pronounced. Sometimes he would shout at the children for no reason. He became a frightening presence in the congregation, and a group went to the leadership team to complain. They wanted him banned from the church.

"We are not feeling safe in our own church," a member said. "Our children are always watching out for him. They're confused by his shouting and try to avoid him. They're not as free as they used to be." "I know we hold hospitality sacred," another person said, "but aren't there boundaries? In offering a safe place for him, *we* no longer feel safe."

Can we put limits on our hospitality? Exclude people if we realize we can no longer nurture them? Do we have the right to say, "Everyone is welcome, but not you?"

INVITATION TO PRACTICE
What would you do in this situation? What limits are you willing to put on your hospitality practice—personal and communal?

Another church had a different dilemma. They had begun as a new congregation in Denver's Capitol Hill neighborhood, known for its marginalized population. Hospitality to the outcast was at the core of their vision. Many people who had not felt accepted in other churches because of dress, sexual orientation, or poverty began to attend. They discovered a welcoming place—a place where they could be authentic, where their souls were fed, and where they could find ways to give back to the wider community.

The creative liturgy, the fine preaching, and the congregational music came to the notice of the wider community. Traditional middle-class people from the suburbs, weary of their own churches, came to see what was going on in this spiritually lively place. At first these visitors were welcomed, but when many of them wanted to make this congregation their church home, the congregation had to look closely at what the new influx of members might mean. They were glad to expand their idea of diversity, but by welcoming these strangers, the congregation's identity was being challenged. Researcher Christine D. Pohl writes of this particular struggle, "While this [challenge] is often enriching, it can occasionally stretch a place beyond recognition."[4] With the possible loss of identity, how will this congregation continue to honor God's call to hospitality?

Welcoming the Stranger Within

As with any spiritual practice, there are gifts and challenges in hospitality, and the role of regular practice is to accustom ourselves to receiving and acknowledging both. When we open our hearts to strangers around us, our souls become ready for the possibility of transformation. The same process we use to open our hearts to strangers in our homes and community settings—our outer world—can be practiced as well in our interior world. Extending hospitality to the strangers within—the parts of ourselves we have forgotten or intentionally excluded—is an integral part of the practice of hospitality. I believe we cannot be truly hospitable to others unless we are willing to welcome our inner outcasts into our own souls.

Rumi, mystical Sufi poet of the ninth century, wrote vividly about the possibilities of welcoming inner strangers. He imagined every human person to be a guesthouse to which unexpected visitors would arrive each morning. Some would be mean or depressed or malicious. Others would bring shame or sorrow. Still others would bring joy and delight. Rumi's advice was to welcome them all, even "to meet them at the door laughing and invite them in." He tells us that no matter who arrives, we must be grateful, "for each has been sent as a guide from beyond."[5]

INVITATION TO PRACTICE

Who are the strangers knocking at your inner door? What
parts of yourself have you excluded or marginalized?
What would be the purpose of inviting them in?

In my own life, and in my work with others, I have experienced
and witnessed how welcoming the stranger within can bring healing
and wholeness. Those parts of ourselves that have been banished, as
well as the feelings that have been excluded, become new in the soft
glow of inclusion. And just like the guests in our homes and places of
worship, they bring unexpected gifts of transformation.

An elderly gentleman I worked with years ago was envious of
people who could sing. Like me, he had been brought up in a home
without music and had never experienced raising his voice in song,
either alone or in community. "My kids used to tell me to just move
my mouth during hymns in church," he told me. "They said I can't
carry a tune."

But he recognized that he had within himself a singing stranger
who had never been acknowledged, so he decided at age seventy-eight
to take singing lessons. "I am so excited," he exclaimed one day. "I've
discovered a whole new way to pray. I have truly become an instrument of God's grace. I still don't sing in church, but I really let go in
the shower."

A woman in her thirties became aware she was avoiding her
friends who were pregnant or had young children. "I'm just too busy,
and we don't have anything in common anymore," she told herself
as she refused hospitality from those she was close to. One day she
passed a pregnant stranger on the street and burst into tears. She was
so startled by her own reaction, she felt moved to look more deeply
at what was happening in her heart and soul. "I've had two miscar-
riages," she told me. "No one knew. I faced the loss alone. I guess I

have been ignoring the part of myself I am now calling the sorrowful stranger, who is still grieving. It's not easy, but I am learning to acknowledge and accept her as an important part of who I am."

This inner work of hospitality carries the same complexities that are present when we offer hospitality to strangers in the outer world. We will probably be ambivalent about the invitation. We may wonder if it will be worth the risk, discomfort, and inconvenience we know comes with welcoming and nurturing the visitor. We doubt the wisdom of inviting in an unknown guest.

When we realize that some aspect of ourselves is knocking on our hearts, we may need to proceed slowly, opening the door just a little and shutting it when necessary. When the guest seems frightening, we can ease our minds and hearts by remembering Rumi's promise that all who come have something to offer. We may not know what gift this stranger is bringing. We may not know what we have been missing until it appears. The only way to receive the gift is to take the risk and welcome the stranger in.

Years ago in an imagination exercise, a horrifying old woman appeared at my inner door. She was old and ugly with no words, only incoherent screeches and howls. I was terrified and did not want to let her in. What gift could she possibly bring me? How could she be a guide from beyond? With help, I found the courage to welcome her. With warmth and acceptance, her image slowly began to change. She did not become beautiful—she remained unsightly and eccentric—but I came to realize that she brought back the gift of creativity that I had buried so long ago.

The many ways we practice hospitality to the strangers within and without have the potential to lead us to a life of hospitality. But there is one giant step still to be taken in the practice of hospitality—the wholehearted willingness to welcome all of life.

Cultivating the Hospitable Heart

The hospitable heart transcends dualities and breaks our habit of seeing the world through either/or eyes. In the Buddhist tradition, this process of letting go of old ways and finding a both/and/everything worldview is called cultivating equanimity. Equanimity is about accepting and welcoming reality just as it is at this moment. We do not label what is happening in the moment as either good or bad; we do not like or dislike, accept or reject, what is happening. We simply open our hearts, inviting all of life to come to visit.

Pema Chodrin, Buddhist teacher and writer, reminds us that cultivating equanimity is a work in progress. "We aspire to spend our lives training in the lovingkindness and courage that it takes to receive whatever appears—sickness, health, poverty, wealth, sorrow, and joy. We welcome and get to know them all."[6]

INVITATION TO PRACTICE

Turn your attention to your breathing. Then take one deep breath imagining that you are breathing in the whole world. What could that depth of welcome mean in your life?

How Are You Called to Practice?

Inviting someone into your home or your place of worship is not usually done as an off-cushion practice. Others involved—family members or the congregation—need to be consulted. But every encounter with friends and strangers can be an opportunity to welcome another into your presence with a smile, a brief greeting, or a wave. Notice when something prevents you from doing even that. Might it be the fear of being caught in the third movement of hospitality—nurturing? That is often what keeps my heart from opening to another.

Attending to and accepting God's invitation to the world created for us might be another way to practice hospitality in the middle of your life. Watch for moments that remind you of this radical hospitality, such as being surprised by awe and wonder at unexpected moments. As you respond to God's many abundant invitations, remember that you are a necessary part of the giving and receiving of hospitality. The practice cannot be completed if you are unable to accept the divine invitation. As you become the honored guest, be aware of ways you are being welcomed and nurtured by creation. In gratitude you may wish to return the favor and be intentional about inviting in and welcoming the holy Presence.

Years after my experience with Orie, I realized that it mirrored the way I often invite, welcome, and nurture God in my life. I can be ambivalent about inviting God's presence. I am apt to welcome the divine Presence with words only, while keeping my heart closed. Then I resist consistently nurturing the Holy in my life. Could this be true for you as well?

Practicing the inner work of hospitality is a lifelong process. You have probably noticed how the inner and outer worlds reflect each other. Wholeness and healing are fostered when we invite in the external stranger, as well as when we include our inner strangers and welcome even our distressing experiences rather than excluding them. This radical act of inclusion is an integral part of the spiritual practice of hospitality. The following extended practices offer two methods to engage this ongoing practice of inner hospitality.

GUIDELINES FOR MORE EXTENDED PRACTICE

WELCOMING THE STRANGER WITHIN

This guided imagery gives you the opportunity to begin exploring the part of yourself that might be knocking at your door, seeking welcome and nurture. You may meet a part of yourself you already know, or you may be surprised. See if you are willing to bring an attitude of curiosity to the meditation.

Find a place where you can sit comfortably and remain alert. Center yourself with your breathing.

⇛ Pay attention to your body, feelings, and thoughts, allowing them to slide to the periphery of your awareness, leaving an open space for your imagination to play.

⇛ Imagine a beautiful setting that is welcoming and safe. It may be some place you have been, or it might be a creation of your imagination. Explore it with all your senses. What does it look like? Are there sounds? How is the temperature? Can you smell anything? Is there food or drink available? As you explore your safe and beautiful place, find a place within it where you can sit comfortably.

⇛ Settle yourself, look around, and invite a part of yourself that has been excluded to join you. You might say, "Who is wanting to be included?" or "Please join me, I need your gift," or "My open heart is waiting for you." After the invitation, wait and see who appears. The image may be clear and come in the form of a person. You might receive an animal or an object. You might simply get a sense of presence or energy. Are you willing to welcome whomever arrives?

⇛ Be aware of your initial response to the one who has arrived. Gaze with compassion, noticing the physical appearance of the guest, the feelings that seem to be present, and the quality of mind. Then gently begin to ask some questions: "What is your name?" "What gift do you bring into my life?" "What do you need from me to feel welcome?"

⇛ Listen to the responses, and continue to dialogue in any way that seems useful and nurturing to both of you. You might imagine offering a welcoming and nurturing gesture.

⇛ Allow the interaction to come to an end. It may end with reconciliation, an impasse, or further questions. Do not force a happy ending. See if you can accept whatever happens.

⇛ When you are ready, let the image of the guest, no longer a stranger, fade. Take some time to reflect on the encounter. How might including this part of yourself help you become more fully alive? You may wish to write about or draw the experience in your journal.

THE WELCOMING PRAYER

The Welcoming Prayer, a practice taught within the Centering Prayer movement, is another way to open our hearts and welcome in our emotional and physical experiences. This is a three-step process in which we *acknowledge* what is going on internally, we *welcome* it, and then we *let it go*. This prayer is not designed to quickly get rid of a distressing situation, but rather to acknowledge and welcome it so deeply that it gradually lets go of us.

I invite you to practice praying with a past experience, one that when remembered still holds sensation and energy. You can use this incident to discover and practice the rhythm and process of the Welcoming Prayer. As the prayer becomes more familiar, you may be able to practice in the middle of your distress or soon after, when the experience is still alive for you.

> Find a place you can sit comfortably without interruption for ten or fifteen minutes. Settle yourself with your breathing, gently letting go of thoughts and expectations.

> Remember a recent time of stress in your life, and picture yourself in the middle of it. Don't think about or analyze the situation, rather feel the bodily and energetic sensations that were part of it.

> Focus and sink into the sensations as fully as you can. Do not try to change anything. Do not use this practice to analyze or justify yourself. Just stay present.

> Grounded in your experience, begin slowly and calmly to say, "Welcome, grief," or "Welcome, pain." If you are unable to name what you are experiencing, you might simply say, "Welcome." Repeat your phrase as many times as you need to truly experience your hospitality of heart.

> When you are ready, but not too soon or too quickly, begin the third step of letting go by saying, "I let go of this grief," or "I let go of this pain," or "I let go of my feelings." It may be wise to add, "I let go of my desire to change this situation."

See if you are willing to experience this ending as a fond farewell, knowing that when the sensations that come with stressful situations return, you will be more familiar with them, more willing to welcome them in, and then to gently let them go.

You may wish to breathe a prayer of gratitude for your experience and possibly draw or write in your journal.

8

THE
PRACTICE
OF SERVICE
Cultivating Generosity, Kindness, and Joy

Don't look for spectacular actions; what is important is the gift of yourselves. It is the degree of love you insert in your deeds.

Mother Teresa of Calcutta

You have probably noticed that the first six chapters of this book are an exploration of interior practices. Caring for our bodies, resting, being silent, experiencing solitude, letting go, and practicing in community are about cultivating internal ways of being fully awake and alive. These contemplative and communal practices focus our gaze inward and invite us to open our hearts and minds to what we discover there.

The previous chapter, the practice of hospitality, is a bridge between the inner and the outer worlds and guides us into the missional practices. When we look inward to discover our desire to welcome the stranger in our own hearts, we are still engaging in contemplative practice. When we look outward to explore inviting others into our lives, we are participating in missional practice. However, this movement from the contemplative to the missional practices is not in one direction only, for we may discover in our experience of missional practice that we are called back to contemplative practice and communal practices, each experience encouraging and supporting the other.

Eboo Patel, a Muslim writer and activist, speaks of the movement from interior contemplative practice to outward, missional practice in the life of Muhammad. Patel knew that the Prophet had received a revelation from God during one of his many solitary pilgrimages to a cave on Mt. Hira. Patel found this piece of history disturbing. As a young man in his twenties, Patel was in love with the world, and he was disappointed to discover that Muhammad was chosen by God because he had been willing to remove himself from everyday life for long periods of time.

Later, when studying his Islamic tradition more extensively, Patel discovered that Muhammad, after being called by God in solitude, brought his revelations down from the mountain into the world. There he preached and counseled, married and had children, and became fully engaged in service to his sisters and brothers. Patel writes, "In the Holy Qur'an, God makes it clear that this was His intention for all human beings. We were made to be His servant and representative on Earth. One of our primary duties is to manifest His mercy here."[1]

This cycle of withdrawal and return is common in the lives of many people who have made major contributions to civilization. Arnold Toynbee, world historian, notes that Confucius, the Buddha, the prophets of Israel and Judah, Jesus, and Socrates all lived this rhythm of contemplation and action. "[Each] had a profound spiritual realization then devoted their lives to service."[2]

We are also called to this cycle of withdrawal and return. By attending to our inner lives through contemplative and communal spiritual practice, we awaken to the power of our spiritual energy flowing outward to the world in the form of loving service.

INVITATION TO PRACTICE
Imagine a line running between your feet dividing the inner
and outer world. Take a deep breath, lift one foot, and place
it firmly in the inner world, and move the other foot to the
outer world. Shift your weight from one foot to the other,
feeling in your body the cycle of withdrawal and return.

When you imagine returning to a hurting world to offer loving service, what comes to mind and heart? Do you think of large projects like the Peace Corps, organizing a homeless shelter for families, or serving on the board of a national nonprofit? Do you look closer to home, to the needs of your family, your friends, or your community? When we return to the world after a time of withdrawal, what will be asked of us? What are we to do? How are we to serve?

When I attempt to answer these questions through analytic thinking, I get stuck in trying to figure out what the practice of serving *means*, rather than feeling my way into what service *is*. Even if we can come up with a clear definition of the practice of service, it will have no life if we have not included the wisdom of our hearts. We need to turn to our lived experience of service to discover its true meaning.

Some clarity arose as I remembered a recent phone call I had received. A friend, someone I see only two or three times a year, called to see if I would accompany her to a presurgical meeting with her new oncologist. "I need another set of ears," she said. "The doctor will be explaining my previous tests and giving me options for treatment. You listen well and are not afraid to ask the hard questions. Will you go with me?"

I told her I would be happy to do so, and we made the necessary plans. I thanked her for asking me. I know her well enough to know that her request came with hesitation, for she is very independent and prides herself on doing things alone. I was honored to be asked.

Her need and my response unlocked the wisdom of my heart in regard to service. I suddenly realized that the practice of service is simply the willingness to respond. In this case, I could willingly and gratefully say yes, for she was calling on my gifts. If she had asked me come to help her do something for which I had no gift—such as decorate her living room—I would have said no, for I have no gift for interior design!

My lived experience of service as response matches the concept of *hineni*, the Hebrew word translated "here I am." *Hineni* is found in multiple places in the Hebrew scriptures, and the Rabbis of the Talmud taught that we respond to God, to the highest call in the universe, when we are present to those whom we love. I think *presence* is the word we might use today to describe this highest calling to first respond to God and from there to respond to others, "Here I am, present to you."

Our gifts are constantly being called forth. When we are present to the needs of others and offer our gifts to individuals, groups, or the wider world, we are practicing service. Sometimes our gifts are being called forth in a clear request, as I received from my friend. Other times our gifts are needed in places and by people who do not ask. Recognizing those needs when we return to the world with our hearts open, we are able to respond to others with integrity. Presbyterian pastor Fredrick Buechner put it this way: "The place God calls you to is the place where your deep gladness and the world's deep hunger meet."[3]

My niece and her husband care deeply about education. Both of them are competent business professionals, but they have chosen to respond to the needs of the city's children by serving on three different boards of charter schools. The gifts they bring to this work are their ability to envision new possibilities and their skills in creating highly functioning organizations. Although board work is sometimes frustrating, they are enlivened by their practice of service.

Sharing our gifts from a loving and generous heart helps us become fully alive. I remember a woman telling me in confidence that her family had been able to give their church enough money to provide the part-time pastor with health insurance. "No one but you knows where the gift came from," she said. Her eyes filled with joyful tears at the telling.

If our practice of service makes us feel resentful or beholden, we are not sharing our gifts as a genuine response to the needs of the world. When we become aware of these feelings, it is time to withdraw for a while and look closely at what we are doing. Sometimes we have said yes to a request out of guilt or with the hope of being liked and appreciated. Other times we may become attached to specific outcomes, and our service becomes controlling or forced. It could be that the need we have responded to does not use our gifts, or we have discovered we don't really have the gifts required for the task. Paying attention to our feelings evoked by our acts of service can guide us in our practice.

INVITATION TO PRACTICE
Remember the feelings associated with your practices of
service. Might some changes be necessary?

As we continue exploring the practice of service, pay attention to what sparks your interest, which practices you feel excited about responding to, which areas you know would not engage your gifts. We will begin with an exploration of off-cushion practices of service and then turn our attention to the call for longer and more intentionally planned responses to the needs of the world.

Hidden Service: The Power of Practices That No One Notices

Richard Foster, author of *Celebration of Discipline*, writes of the goodness that comes when we serve others without being noticed. These are not acts done in secret, but rather are ways of relating to other people that slip by their awareness. However, the results of these acts of service impact both the individual and the community in which they take place.

One hidden service we all have the opportunity to practice is watching carefully what we say about others. How easy it is to engage in casual gossip, cast judgment on another person's ideas or behaviors, and compare other people's attributes and limitations. "She is much smarter than her boss." "He seems to have lost his creative spark." "Did you notice how inappropriately she dresses?" "That family is very judgmental of others."

The Dalai Lama has been known to teach that before we speak we should ask ourselves if what we are about to say is true, kind, and necessary. I often wonder whether there would be much talk at all if everyone adhered to these guidelines! We are so accustomed to half-truths and embellishments, unkind words, and unnecessary babble that we often become inattentive to our own words, not noticing how our speech affects others and our environment.

One year a friend gave up gossip for Lent. She wanted to watch her own tongue but also wanted to notice when she participated in gossip simply by being willing to listen to it. She first recognized how often she was tempted to speak unkindly about someone. She was surprised how prevalent this way of speaking was where she worked. As she became more aware of the swirl of gossip and her temptation to join in, she found herself able to interrupt another person's tale by gently saying, "I really don't want to hear that."

INVITATION TO PRACTICE

Watch the next temptation to gossip, and see if you are
willing to hold your tongue.

Sometimes, as in the case of avoiding gossip, the spiritual practice is refraining from speech. But sometimes hard truths need to be spoken, and the spiritual practice is to speak intentionally and compassionately.

When I was teaching elementary school, I would have been irresponsible not to tell parents about their child's difficulty with reading, disrespectful behavior, or any other problem I was observing in the classroom. It would have been easier to say nothing. To remain silent would have been avoiding my responsibility as a teacher and would have been a disservice to both the parents and child. Withholding important information about their child would not be giving them the information they needed to be responsible parents.

When faced with this situation, I practiced speaking to the parents kindly and gently, giving examples of the problems I had seen. I tried not to be defensive when the parents questioned my judgment. I let go of any expectation that the parents would hear what I had to say or offer to cooperate in solving the problem. I simply knew I needed to speak the truth in love (Ephesians 4:15).

Another hidden service is listening compassionately to others. We examined the art of listening in our exploration of silence when we practiced listening to our hearts and to God. We can take this practice into the company of others, finding ways to listen deeply to someone else's story. Have you ever been filled with thoughts and emotions that needed to be verbalized? Have you ever longed to tell your story to a loving heart? This experience can help us know how deep listening is a spiritual practice.

A number of years ago, after a disturbing family incident, I called my sister to talk about it. We live only five minutes apart, and she suggested I come over instead of using the telephone. When I arrived, she was in the kitchen, and I began to share my experience. Although I began by speaking casually, she picked up on the depth of my emotions. She put down her tasks, took me to her bedroom, and closed the door. I burst into tears. I hadn't even known how badly I needed her compassionate, listening heart. Deep listening is a service, for as a friend of mine said about her therapist, "When he listens, I hear what I say, and I know what I feel."

To listen in this healing way, we must be able to listen silently and attentively, resisting the temptation to interrupt. I have noticed three different patterns of interruptions that occur frequently in our culture. These interruptions are not meant to be rude; we are usually trying to be helpful. We don't realize that the story we are listening to has a rhythm of its own that may be guiding the person more deeply into his or her experience. Anytime we break in with unnecessary words, we lift the other person back to the surface of his or her story, and an opportunity for deep listening has passed.

We often interrupt a story with suggestions on how to fix whatever problem is being shared. Have you ever started to pour out your heart to a friend about the injustice you are experiencing at work, to be immediately interrupted with advice? Your listener may have ideas on what you might say to your boss or what you shouldn't say to your boss. He might advise you to quit your job. She might suggest bringing in a consultant. However helpful the advice may seem, the story has been short-circuited.

Interjecting our own story into a conversation is another way we interrupt. I think we believe that by sharing our experience we are letting the other person know that we understand what they are going through. But our stories steal the experiences away from the original storyteller and prevent him or her from exploring their own unique feelings. When a friend was facing knee surgery, she told me she had stopped telling people about it. "I've heard so many stories of other people's knee replacements," she said, "but no one has listened to my feelings of fear as well as my hope for being mobile again."

INVITATION TO PRACTICE
Pay attention to your own patterns of interruption, and
again see if you are willing to hold your tongue.

The pattern of interruption I have the hardest time resisting is the desire to break in to a story for more information or unnecessary details. I want to know how many people were at the party, or the name of her cousin, or how long the plane flight took. If I don't understand exactly what is being said, I interrupt for clarity. When I am tempted to ask these questions, I return to a lesson taught to me by my younger stepson.

When Paul was in the third grade, he came home from school one day very agitated, found me in the kitchen, and began to talk. He was walking around the room as fast as he was speaking, and I understood very little of what he was saying. I kept silent and out of his way, and after about five minutes he slowed down, and then he stopped. In great relief, he hugged me and said, "Jane, you are a great listener," and ran from the room.

A final hidden service is quite paradoxical—it is the practice of being willing to be served. Service cannot happen if there is no recipient, yet we are often reluctant to accept the help being offered. A teenager gets up to give you his seat on the bus and you say, "No, thank you." The neighbor offers to bring your family a meal when you have been sick, and you say, "Oh, that's not necessary." Your grocery bag splits in the parking lot and someone comes to help. "Thank you," you say. "I can take care of it myself."

INVITATION TO PRACTICE
The next time someone offers to serve you, notice if
you can receive graciously. How does that feel?

The Gospel of John in the Christian scriptures contains a story about the common reluctance to accept service from others. It is the night before Jesus's betrayal, and he has gathered his disciples for the Passover meal. After teaching them about his coming death, he gets up from the table, takes off his outer robe, and ties a towel around himself in the manner of a servant. He then pours water in a basin and begins to wash the feet of his disciples. While the others accept his ministrations, Simon Peter questions him. "Lord, are you going to wash my feet?" he asks. Jesus offers Peter an explanation on why his service to him is important, but Peter still does not understand, and he says adamantly, "You will never wash my feet" (John 13:4–8).

Peter finally agrees to allow Jesus to serve him in this way, but I think, like Peter, we are all ambivalent about accepting loving service from others. There is a fierce independence in our culture that makes us believe we are less than whole if we need help from others. By refusing help, we are denying our natural state of interdependence.

One day, walking in my neighborhood, I came across a teenager sitting on the curb weeping. I looked away and went around her, thinking to give her privacy, and then I stopped and turned back. "Can I help you?" I asked. She looked away and shook her head. "I'm OK," she mumbled. I left her sitting there, wondering whether she truly wanted to be alone or was actually resisting the offering of help out of habit or pride. I wanted to sit beside her and offer comfort, but I honored her response.

When our offer of help is refused, we often refrain from reaching out in another situation, fearing it will not be welcome. It can be awkward when another interprets our help as intrusive or demeaning. But what if a person needs help and we withhold it out of fear? A colleague in a wheelchair she self-propels told me that nothing feels better than when a stranger comes up behind her, asks if he might be of assistance, then takes the handles of her chair, and gives her a helpful push. "I know people hesitate," she said. "Many of us take great pride in our independence and doing for ourselves. But I feel blessed when someone notices my struggle and reaches out."

INVITATION TO PRACTICE
Watch for opportunities to reach out to help someone.
Pay attention to your inner dialogue as to whether to
offer assistance or not.

A home health care nurse told me she had discovered that her elderly patients who could graciously receive help had a higher quality of life than those who resisted her care. "Irrespective of the amount of money available or the seriousness of the illness, those who accepted my service seemed to be happier and more hopeful," she told me. "I know it's not a scientific study, but my observations are leading me to practice accepting help now when I am still young. When I need care, I will know how to receive it."

I am sure there are other hidden services besides the three I have mentioned—watching our tongues, listening to others, and accepting service from others. Watch for an opportunity to be kindhearted to friends and strangers in whatever way seems called for, and you will have discovered another spiritual practice. All of these ways of serving others are the means of *tikkun olam*, the Hebrew words for "repairing the world." In the Jewish tradition, secular practices, along with proscribed religious obligations, are holy acts that have the power to restore peace on earth. We are all called to this sacred way of living in the world—to acts of service both small and large.

The Practice of Discernment: Deciding Who, Where, and How to Serve

In certain periods of life, many of us may find that engaging in hidden service is not enough. We feel called to engage the needs of the world in a more formal and intentional way. You might be invited to serve on the board of an organization promoting interfaith dialogue. You could feel ready to make a commitment to your neighborhood school to tutor young children in reading or arithmetic. A story on National Public Radio on the plight of homeless families touches your heart, and you want to get involved in your own city. Service practices such as these can often be integrated into your daily life; however, some projects may call you to a significant lifestyle change.

People of all ages decide to enter the Peace Corps and give two years of their lives to service. Others work through religious organizations to go to places of need in times of disaster. We hear stories of people in lucrative jobs who leave their comfort and security to share their skills with those in need. If we feel called to this more extensive practice of service, how do we decide how, where, and whom to serve?

Remember Fredrick Buechner's words, "The place God calls you to is the place where your deep gladness and the world's deep hunger meet." This beautiful statement certainly provides direction, but how do we know where our deep gladness resides? How do we know which of the world's deep hungers we are to engage? These are issues we address in the practice of spiritual discernment.

I used to think that discernment was problem solving with a spiritual dimension. I thought we were simply to include God in the process of rational decision making. We might consult others and gather as much information as possible and then pray for clarity. Or we could list everything in favor of one possibility, list everything against it, and then pray for guidance. I have discovered that discernment is much more than learning to make wise decisions.

The practice of discernment is the willingness to listen deeply, engaging the body, mind, and feelings to help us pay attention to the possibilities and choices before us. It is more about being receptive than about taking action. Spiritual writer Wendy Wright imagines discernment as the movement of the sunflower turning to the sun. Another image she uses is that discernment is like being grasped in the spirit's arms and led in the rhythms of an unknown dance.[4]

INVITATION TO PRACTICE
Remember a time when you were in the process of
making a decision and slowly, almost imperceptibly,
found yourself turning toward one option.
What was your experience of being invited by the
spirit to dance to an unfamiliar rhythm?

When exploring options for the practice of service, most of us would prefer quick, clear answers rather than practicing the patience that true discernment calls for. A friend of mine expressed this desire when she exclaimed, "I wish God still spoke in burning bushes. Then I could know I was making the right choice."

We would all like to receive that clarity, but in my experience it happens rarely. I have heard some people report that they knew in a flash that they had to go on a mission trip, organize the local church to serve homeless families, or paint a series of scenes that depicted the possibility of a just and peaceful world. I have never received that kind of clarity in relation to my spiritual practice of service. In fact, I have experienced absolute clarity only twice—once when I knew for certain I needed to leave my first marriage, and the other when against all logic I enrolled in seminary. Not a lot of immediate clarity in seventy-two years! But when I look back over my life and take time to reflect on the choices I have made, I am able to see a pattern of guidance. It seems that without realizing it, I have been allowing the spirit to lead me—it seems I have been following the sun.

INVITATION TO PRACTICE
What patterns of guidance have you experienced in your own life? How might the spirit have been active in your decisions?

When you are in the middle of discerning the way you feel called to practice service, and are not aware of any nudges from the spirit, you may wish to engage what I call the "step-by-step" method of discernment. In this process you take the first step toward one option, even if you are not sure it is the right one. This risky first step allows you to stop and listen in a new way, for now you have more information. Then you take another step and stop and listen. Each period of pausing and resting may provide you with a little more clarity.

A man considering a job with a nonprofit was in a quandary about whether he wanted to work at that particular place. As we explored his feelings, I realized he had not yet applied for the job! By not taking the first step he did not have enough information to facilitate the discernment process. More information would help him listen more intently for holy guidance. By taking the risk and applying for the job, even when he was not sure it was what he wanted, he might become clearer about the workings of that institution and whether he belonged there. If he applied and was not offered the job, he would know that that position was no longer an option, and he would be able to move on to other possibilities.

INVITATION TO PRACTICE
What are the small steps that you might take to get more information about a choice you are facing in your life? Are you willing to do that even if you are not sure it is the "right" step?

Bearing Witness: No Need to Fix Anything

In our eagerness to be of service to others and the world, we are sometimes overwhelmed with matters of need, oppression, and injustice that cannot be fixed. A visit to Auschwitz or the Cambodian killing fields may defy any action but tears. Watching hundreds of people being turned away from a shelter because there are no more beds may leave us feeling helpless. Reading about the number of children in this affluent country who go to bed hungry can make us despair. We are often tempted to skip over the story, turn away from the pain of others, and avoid visiting sites of violence and genocide. But if we are to practice being of service to the world, we must have the courage to see reality in all its guises. We must bear witness to what has gone before and to the pain and injustices that continue today.

Bearing witness is not only having the courage to see. When we bear witness, we must also find the courage to feel. Bearing witness is what you are doing when in your grief you sit silently with a dying friend or when you listen with loving attention to the difficult and painful story of another. You might bear witness more publicly if you were to stand outside a prison, join a prayer service in a migrant camp, or sit in the shadow of government buildings.

INVITATION TO PRACTICE
Remember a time when you were able to bear witness.
How did it feel to see and to feel and not run away?

Bearing witness is another example of *hineni* ("here I am"), mentioned earlier as a way we practice service. The willingness to simply respond to a situation by "standing here" is about living with questions rather than answers, mystery rather than certainty, not knowing rather than knowing. In Zen Buddhism, this way of being in the world is called living with beginner's mind. Beginner's mind allows us to simply show up to be present to the situation with no idea of what will happen, what we should do, or how to change anything. Some would say we are doing nothing, but I believe that by showing up and seeing and feeling the situation with our minds and hearts, our very presence can open the way for the power of holy love and mercy to affect the situation. Through our witness, divine energy has the power to transform hearts and lives. Sometimes doing nothing lovingly allows something to happen.

Many Hands Make Light Work: Practicing Service in Community

The practice of service takes us into the world and into community. Some acts of service are done alone, while others require the presence of like-minded souls. One person can sit silently at the hospital bed or reach out to another in need, but it would be foolish to try to operate a soup kitchen by yourself.

Like the practice of hospitality, the movement from solitary service to practicing service as part of community has its gifts and its challenges. When we serve with others, we are supported and encouraged by their presence and their actions. Tasks can be divided up, and each person can serve in the area of his or her gifts. On the building sites of Habitat for Humanity, you will see some people high on the roof with hammers, others carrying supplies to where they are needed. Some people issue orders, while others follow directions. On the sidelines, people gather to prepare snacks and drinks for the workers, and they cheer when progress is made.

INVITATION TO PRACTICE
When have you worked harmoniously with others to accomplish a task you could not have accomplished alone? What feelings were present in this endeavor?

The image of groups of people working in harmony toward the same goal is inspiring. However, getting to that point may be difficult. In any community there are differences of opinions as to what should be done and how it should be accomplished. Many ideas and voices need to be heard, and decisions will have to be made that may not make everyone happy. Conflict over leadership can emerge, and power struggles may result. Working together in service to others calls us to our earlier practices, particularly the practices of listening and letting go.

As a group begins meeting to make plans for a service project, more will be accomplished when all present are able to listen to one another with open hearts. When we listen in this respectful manner, we are engaging in dialogue rather than discussion or debate.

In debate, we listen and speak with the sole goal of winning. We present our ideas to be convincing—both with our choice of words and our delivery. We listen for weakness in our opponents' remarks and counter them with conviction. We are in the conversation to win.

Discussion can simply be polite debate. We may not pick apart the ideas of those who disagree with us. We may not raise our voices or point our fingers, but we are still intent on winning. As others speak, we don't really hear their words, rather we are planning what to say next when we have the chance. We want the group's opinion and the final decision to affirm our own preconceived ideas and plans.

In dialogue, we enter into conversation to truly hear one another. We begin with the willingness for our hearts to be changed by what we hear. Dialogue includes periods of silence so we can reflect on what has been said. We do not interrupt or talk over each other. No one preaches or lectures; everyone shares from the heart. Dialogue is a way to practice discernment in a group and often needs to precede the practice of service in community.

INVITATION TO PRACTICE
When have you experienced true dialogue? What was accomplished through this kind of conversation?

The practice of letting go is an integral part of the dialogue process. To listen with the knowledge that our hearts might be changed means we may have to let go of cherished beliefs. To realize that the community may decide to do something different from what we desire necessitates our letting go of our plans and envisioned outcome. If we are willing to interact in community in this way, the service project that emerges from the dialogue can be carried forth without resentment or attachment to success. We will be able to serve with love.

Responding to the Needs of Mother Earth

No one needs the loving service by the whole human community more than our Mother Earth. The apostle Paul wrote in his letter to the Christian community in Rome, "We know that that the whole creation has been groaning as in the pains of childbirth" (Romans 8:22). Although this was written almost two thousand years ago, the earth and all her creatures continue to groan and cry out in need. Temperatures are rising, poisons pollute the waters, forests are being decimated, and whole species are disappearing. Creation needs our help.

The devastation occurring on the planet can seem so overwhelming that we turn away in hopelessness, wondering what an individual or a small group can do. We tend to want governments or large corporations to tackle the problem and make things right. Although it will surely take the world community to heal the planet, we must not ignore our own responsibility.

Joining an environmental action group, riding your bike instead of driving, planting trees, turning off the lights when we leave home, recycling our trash, and conserving water are all small acts that we can attend to on a daily basis. These actions may seem small, but "almost anything you do will seem insignificant," wrote Mahatma Gandhi, "but it is very important you do it."[5]

INVITATION TO PRACTICE
Make a commitment to do one thing this day
to help heal the earth.

How Are You Called to Practice?

As you reflect on what your practice of service is to be, remember Mother Teresa's advice at the beginning of this chapter not to look for spectacular actions but rather to focus on the love you can insert in your acts of service, whether in your family, your community, or the wider world. You might also pay attention to your own "deep gladness." When and where do you feel most fully alive?

The practice of service can become a way of life when you move through your world encountering others who may need your help, as well as those who wish to serve you. How will you respond to the needs you witness as well as the kindness that may be offered? As in all the earlier practices, service calls us to wake up and pay attention, but in this case we are called also to see and respond to others. Who needs listening to? Where might kind, true, and necessary words be called for? How might you become more willing to receive help from others, thus becoming more aware of your natural state of interdependence?

Is it the time in your life when you want to give yourself more fully to the service of others? Or change the focus of your service? A young activist realized that with her marriage and birth of twins, her service needed to be at home, rather than in the wider world. She felt a loss in letting go of her public witness but realized that her family was now her first priority. "I may go back to working for justice in the larger community at another time," she said. "Right now I belong at home."

The call to service requires a discerning heart. With so much need in our world, we cannot serve everyone and everywhere. We must choose, and we must accept our limitations and choices. Feeling guilty about not doing more serves no one. For this reason, one of the extended practices for this chapter is designed to help you spend some quality time in discernment.

As you continue to explore the practice of service, you might be guided by these wise words from the Indian poet Rabindranath Tagore:

> *I slept and dreamt that life was joy.*
> *I awoke and saw that life was service.*
> *I acted and behold, service was joy.*[6]

GUIDELINES FOR MORE EXTENDED PRACTICE

LETTING THE MUD SETTLE AND BECOMING STILL

This guided imagery exploring the practice of discernment begins with the wisdom of the Chinese classic the Tao Te Ching, in which we find these two evocative questions:

> *Do you have the patience to wait till your mud settles and the water is clear?*
> *Can you remain unmoving till the right action arises by itself?*[7]

- After you have read and pondered these questions, find a quiet place where you can sit quietly and not be disturbed. Center yourself with your breathing, and then gently pay attention to what is happening in your body, feelings, and mind. When you are ready, allow this content to slide to the periphery of your mind and heart, leaving an open space for your imagination to play.

- I invite you to imagine a pond. You might place it in a meadow, in the forest, or at the foot of a mountain. Create for yourself a beautiful scene.

- When you have a sense of your pond, see if you are willing to approach the pond and look into its clear still water. Maybe you can see below the surface. Maybe it is reflecting the light. It could be too dark to see. But you know it is still; you can feel the stillness.

- Suddenly you become aware of a slight disturbance in the water. The movement begins gently, then increases in tempo. You realize the still, clear pond is slowly becoming clouded with swirling mud. The thrashing has disturbed the peace of the pond.

- As you watch this change, pay attention to how you feel. Simply notice; do not attempt to analyze.

❧ As you sit watching, you realize that the pond is growing quiet again, the mud is beginning to settle, the water is growing clear. How does this change make you feel? Notice any difference in your feelings from the previous change when the water went from still to disturbed and murky.

❧ Now see if you might be willing to take this newly discovered stillness of the pond into your own body. Where does the stillness rest? How do you experience the quiet? What feelings accompany the stillness?

❧ Allow something—a thought, a feeling, or a physical sensation—to disturb the stillness in your own soul, to agitate the water, to stir up the mud. Feel this agitation in your body. Notice where the movement began. How do you experience the thrashing? What feelings are now present?

❧ Once again, allow the mud to settle. Feel the stillness begin to return. In the peace that comes, hold these questions gently: Do I have the patience to wait till my mud settles and the water is clear? Can I remain unmoving till the right action arises by itself?

❧ Stay with the questions and the experience as long as you wish. Then allow the image to fade—at the same time staying connected to the experience.

❧ When you are ready, bring your attention back into your room, moving your body in the chair, your feet on the floor. Gently open your eyes and reflect on what you have learned—about yourself and the practice of discernment in your own life. Do you see ways that this image could guide you in your practice of service?

❧ You can continue to practice with this image of the still pond at any time during your day. When you feel the agitation, simply acknowledge that the mud is being stirred up. When you are ready, imagine the pond calming and the mud settling. Feel it in your body and spirit. Who knows what clarity may arise!

LISTENING WITH AN OPEN HEART— INCLUDING SILENCE IN THE CONVERSATION

Most of us know the joy of being listened to and often wish to serve others by attending to their stories. Deep listening takes practice, and this reflection is designed to prepare your heart so you are ready when you sense the need of another to be heard. For this practice you will need to ask a trusted friend to tell you a story you can listen to. You will need a clock or watch, to help you keep track of time, and paper and pencil for both of you.

- Find a place where you won't be interrupted and can both sit comfortably for about twenty minutes.

- Begin by telling your friend about the practice of deep listening and what you are hoping to learn from this experience together. You might want to read him or her these guidelines to clarify the process.

- Then sit quietly together with your eyes closed, quieting your minds and hearts. When you are ready, invite your friend to begin speaking—to tell a story, to explain a situation, or to explore an issue—whatever feels right. He or she is to share for seven minutes while you simply listen.

- Your task during this time is to notice the many ways you are tempted to interrupt the story. If you had not made the covenant of silence, what would you be asking or saying as you listen to your friend?

- At the end of seven minutes, take about three minutes to make notes to yourselves. You can write down your temptations to interrupt. Did you want to tell your friend what to do, share a similar story of your own, or ask unnecessary questions? Your friend can write about what it was like to be listened to in this way.

- You can end the practice here if you wish and share with each other what you noticed in those seven minutes. Or you can continue for five more minutes.

If you choose to go on, you may begin to ask questions to guide your friend to a deeper place in relation to the story. See if you are willing to have brief periods of silence as part of this conversation, leaving time between questions and responses.

When these five minutes are up, take another three minutes for each of you to write about what you noticed during this time period. How were the two periods of speaking similar? If there was a difference, which time was more comfortable? Do you know why?

End your time together with some informal sharing, noticing again the way you listen.

9

THE
FRUITS
OF PRACTICE
Living Gratefully, Humbly, and Compassionately

The only way to judge [your practice] is by its long-range fruits: whether in daily life you enjoy greater peace, humility and charity.

Father Thomas Keating

The mystics tell us that what happens during prayer is not important. What counts are the fruits of our practice that slowly become visible in our lives. I have chosen to explore gratefulness, humility, and compassion as the fruits of spiritual practice, but they are in no way the only possibilities. Peace might be another fruit, or patience, or hope. In addition, rather than waiting for compassion to flower, you might decide to begin an intentional gratitude practice and realize that the fruit of that practice of gratefulness is an urge to service. You may have already realized that one of the earlier practices yields yet another fruit, as when caring for your body guides you toward living restfully. When practicing hospitality, you might experience patience beginning to grow. There is no list of practices and no list of fruits; rather, any practice we choose can bear fruit in our lives. The spiritual practices and the fruits of practice intersect and interact to help us wake up to the fullness of life.

INVITATION TO PRACTICE
How have you noticed your spiritual practices bearing
fruit in other parts of your life?

The fruits of practice are not goals, for a goal assumes a place in the future that we are striving for and have not yet reached. Rather, the fruits of practice are the unfolding of beneficial qualities that we begin to notice in our lives. Many of the fruits come as surprises, bringing us new ways to see and experience a life of fullness.

Doing anything without a clear goal or purpose is not the way of our culture. Most of us have been taught to find our purpose, set a goal, and put all our energy and talent behind making it happen. This often occurs as well in the spiritual life. Common goals for spiritual practice may be to have a good experience, to feel better, or to achieve a peaceful heart. When we sit in meditation, we want to arise refreshed. When we dance our prayers, we hope to connect to our deeper selves. When we journal, we expect to receive insights that can guide our choices. We want to see results, and we want those results to be pleasing.

When I was teaching seminary students a variety of prayer forms, I would ask them to practice a different method each week. Often a student would return to the next class and report, "That prayer really worked!" When I asked what she meant by "worked," she might reply that the prayer form seemed natural, that it was comfortable, or that she felt better as a result of the practice. I would then ask the students if feeling comfortable and more at peace was why they practiced. What did they think about the practices that agitated them, caused discomfort, or led to confusion? Were those practices that "didn't work"? Should they ignore them?

INVITATION TO PRACTICE
What do you believe is the purpose of spiritual practice?
What drew you to this book in the first place?

Many people, when asked the purpose of spiritual practice, might say that they practice to become clear-minded. Others could declare they are seeking enlightenment. Still others wish to become more spiritually mature. Whatever the specific response, we usually practice to get somewhere other than where we are. However, many spiritual teachers will tell us that there is nowhere to go, for we are already there. We are what we are seeking. We are right now who we want to become. The true purpose of spiritual practice is to wake up to that reality, to accept that all there is, is now.

If our reason to practice is to wake up—to life, to who we truly are, and to the present moment—we must be prepared to be disillusioned. We have to let go of the ways we had always thought the world worked. Facing life exactly as it is does not always feel good. Recognizing that we have been living with false assumptions about who we are can be painful. If our lives have been about striving toward something beyond the present moment, giving up that orientation to the future can be frightening. Why would anyone want to engage in practices that bring forth doubt, pain, and fear?

I believe that under these questions and doubts there is in all of us the desire to wake up. Even as we resist, there is a force within calling us to spiritual practices, the fruits of which can be lives of fullness and authenticity. If we have been listening to ourselves, we may have heard that still, small voice wondering if the life we are living is all there is. We could have felt the urge to let go of habits that restrict us. We might have seen in others what could be possible in our own lives.

If we are already who we are meant to be, if being awake is our essential nature, then there is no need to strive. The struggle comes when we resist waking up to that reality. We have all kinds of excuses for staying asleep. "Life as it is may not be perfect, but it is familiar." "Who would I be if I am not who I was?" "What in the world would my family think!"

INVITATION TO PRACTICE
What are the ways you resist waking up to what is?
What excuses do you make?

Although we may long to be fully awake, once and for all, most of us experience waking up as a lifelong process. Spiritual practices help us have moments of awakening, glimpses of new ways of being and living, and hints of what being truly alive might mean. Then we go back to sleep, but the possibility of wakefulness lingers, and we may turn once more to those practices that touch our souls and refresh our spirits.

As we practice in a variety of ways, we may begin to see subtle signs of the fruits of our practice. We may not be fully awake, but we notice that we are seeing others and ourselves differently—with less judgment and more compassion. We notice that life seems more surprising and we are more in touch with awe and wonder and are moved to gratefulness in all things. We may realize that humility has crept into our being and we have found strength in our weaknesses and hope in our imperfection.

These three practices of gratefulness, humility, and compassion, which we will explore in depth, are commonly thought of as fruits of other forms of spiritual practice. They may also be practiced intentionally (I offer some practices at the end of this chapter), but I invite you to first explore them as fruits, noticing how they become more apparent in your life as you engage in a variety of other spiritual practices.

The Experience of Living Gratefully

I don't think I was very grateful as a child. With all the material and emotional gifts I was given, I tended to focus on what I didn't have. I was disappointed in our modest family vacations, desiring instead to travel somewhere exotic. I wished for my father to be home more than he was. I longed for a best friend. I really wanted a room of my own.

I had been taught to say "thank you" at the appropriate moments and responded with those words automatically. I wrote my thank-you notes on time, even when I didn't like the gift that had been sent. I expressed gratitude in my prayers, but these words rarely came from a heart full of thanksgiving, and more often from the teachings I had received about how to pray. I had been taught that it was good to give God thanks and praise. So I would thank God for my mother and father and sister, my grandmother, my dog—all without much thought.

When I was a teenager, I was very confused by Saint Paul's admonition in his letter to the Thessalonians to "give thanks in all circumstances" (1 Thessalonians 5:18). How could I possibly be grateful for not having a date to the prom? Why would I give thanks for being turned down at one of the colleges of my choice? There was no place for gratitude when I heard the news that a classmate had been murdered.

Not until I went to seminary did I realize that Paul was not teaching us to be thankful *for* all things, but rather to give thanks *in* all things. For the first time, living gratefully became a possibility. Although I could never be grateful for my father's early death, I was thankful for the loving support my family received from individuals and the community. When recovering from serious illness caused by the West Nile virus, I became grateful for every new accomplishment—sitting up by myself, drying my hair, walking out the front door. Every step seemed a tiny miracle. After the attacks on the World Trade Center and the Pentagon in 2001, the Muslim community of Denver began receiving threats. Soon hundreds of people from all walks of life arrived at the mosque to encircle it with love and protection. I was grateful for the outpouring of compassion.

INVITATION TO PRACTICE
When have you experienced the challenge of
"giving thanks in all circumstances"?

Gratefulness can grow from new insights, from new experiences, and through grace. A variety of spiritual practices can also help gratitude to flower. But sometimes people need a specific practice to cultivate a grateful heart. Over ten years ago I suggested to one of my directees that she begin a gratitude journal. She was in the middle of a very difficult work situation, and the struggle was wearing her out. She needed help shifting her focus from despair to blessing. Each evening, before bed, she would look back over her day and write down things she was grateful for. She looked for little things such as the smile of a colleague, the lack of traffic on her commute home, a phone call from her sister, ice cream for dessert. She was struggling to find ways to give thanks in all circumstances, and the journal reminded her that it was possible.

Recently she and her partner both retired and moved across the country to be near her children and grandchildren. As she told me about selling their home, finding a place to live in a new community, the packing and the unpacking, and all the stress of the transition, she said how blessed they both felt. The choice to move was a good one, their relationship was deepening, and they were excited about new opportunities.

"I found my old gratitude journal," she said. "It was in one of the boxes I just unpacked. I thought it might be a good idea to begin writing in it again, so I placed it on my nightstand. But I haven't touched it. I wonder why." I told her I wasn't surprised she was letting it rest. She had begun that journal when she had to hunt for things to be grateful for, and now gratitude had become integrated into her daily life. In the midst of a major move with all the potential for problems and discontent, she was able to see blessings all around her. She didn't need to search for them—they were everywhere.

Sometimes we are blind to the blessings that surround us and then stumble across a reminder of the way we can live gratefully. During my morning solitary walk earlier this week, I began to sneeze. Not just once but three times in a row. A passing mailperson called out, "Bless you!" I thanked him and said how lovely it was to receive a morning blessing. He replied, "Every day is a blessing." Here was a man not only living gratefully, he was sharing his blessings with others.

INVITATION TO PRACTICE
Put down the book, breathe deeply, and say to yourself,
"Today, just as it is, is a blessing."

Surprise Is the Wisdom of a Grateful Heart

Brother David Steindl-Rast believes that surprise is the starting point of gratefulness. "Through surprise our inner eyes are opened to the amazing fact that everything is gratuitous," he writes. "Nothing at all can be taken for granted. And if it cannot be taken for granted, it is a gift."[1] When I first read these words years ago, Brother David made me rethink what I had always assumed about surprises. Instead of experiencing surprises as reminders that all of life is a gift, my history contained many surprises that were big and dramatic events—my sister's cancer diagnosis, the sudden breakup of a relationship, and the cancellation of a trip due to illness.

Because of these negative experiences, I did everything in my power to avoid surprises. Soon after Jim and I were married, my young stepsons enjoyed sneaking up on me when I was attending to something else, or jumping from behind a chair to startle me. They liked to hear me scream, but they finally got the message that I really didn't enjoy those surprises. "Don't ever give me a surprise party," I warned Jim. "It will make me miserable."

What I hadn't acknowledged was how much I was missing by guarding against all kinds of surprises. My inner eyes had been blind to the fact that the most ordinary events are actually quite surprising. The sun comes up every morning! Spring comes every year! By taking much of life for granted, I had stopped seeing the wonder of the first snow, the miracle of clean water, the pleasure of an unexpected call from an old friend, or the thrill of a perfect turn of phrase I discovered in a poem. All gift; nothing to be taken for granted; a new way of seeing and being in the world. When we experience everything to be surprising, even the most ordinary detail, we are filled with awe and wonder and gratefulness. (I still don't want a surprise party!)

INVITATION TO PRACTICE
Stop reading and look around you. What ordinary things do
you see or hear that you realize are actually surprising?

You may see a connection between your growing ability to live gratefully and some earlier practices. Did caring for your body lead you to gratitude? Did engaging in communal spiritual practices or service open your grateful heart? As you begin to see the ordinary as surprising and even welcome the totally unexpected events tossed your way, you may realize that you are living more gratefully and more joyfully. Brother David suggests that when we notice joyful people who are grateful, we are apt to assume that they are grateful for their joy. But he thinks otherwise. He believes their joy springs from their gratefulness. "We hold the key to lasting happiness in our own hands," he writes. "For it is not joy that makes us grateful; it is gratitude that makes us joyful."[2]

Humility—the Forgotten Virtue

If gratefulness is at the heart of waking up and being truly, joyfully alive, I believe that humility is an integral part of the experience of gratitude. How can we not be humbled by the wonder around us, the abundance of gifts, the surprises that await us? But humility is often ignored and certainly not desired or sought after in the same way, or with the same frequency, that we may desire other virtues such as honesty, patience, courage, or generosity. And yet when we are with truly humble people, we know the blessings their presence can bring to us.

When working with a directee on his issues of pride and arrogance, I asked him what humility looked like. Did he know of any humble people? He immediately named Mother Teresa and Gandhi, but I was looking for someone closer to home—a friend or acquaintance. He could think of no one. He was surprised when he realized that humility was not a quality that he admired, so he had never looked for it in others or himself.

INVITATION TO PRACTICE
Who in your life is a model of humility? How do you
know that they are humble?

One person that comes to my mind as a model of humility is Father Henri Nouwen, a wounded healer, a wise and troubled man. Nouwen left his prestigious position at Harvard to live at a L'Arche community that serves people with severe mental and physical disabilities. He realized that all the attention and adoration he was receiving for his writing and teaching were taking a great toll on his soul. He needed to let go of his position and be faithful to Jesus's teaching that "for those who want to save their life will lose it, and those who lose their life for my sake, and for the sake of the Gospel, will save it" (Mark 8:35). Nouwen "lost" his position to save his life.

Although he left academia, Nouwen continued to teach and lead retreats. At one such gathering he told the group about the paradoxical event of being awarded a silver medal in humility by a diocese of the Catholic Church. He was embarrassed by being singled out and felt awkward in accepting it. What does a humble man do with a silver medal for humility? Nouwen told the group that all he could do was gently poke fun at the paradox. So instead of simply thanking the bishop, he raised his hands in pleasure and cried, "All I can say is, I'm going for the gold!"

The Gracious Gift of Humility

How do we become humble? I have heard Father Richard Rohr, founder of the Center for Action and Contemplation, say that he prays for at least one humiliation a day to keep him humble. Small daily humiliations like saying something stupid, or forgetting an appointment, or tripping over our own feet can help us grow in humility. These humiliations are inner experiences and are simply a part of everyday life. We come to them by our own mistakes. I think they help us grow in humility, for they are constant reminders of our imperfections.

However, when humiliation comes from the outside, from people who use humiliation to punish or manipulate, the virtue of humility is not fostered. Parents and teachers who intentionally humiliate children to rid them of the sin of pride or those in authority who humiliate others for the sake of control can cause deep wounds that hamper growth and freedom. Sometimes these wounds can be healed and transformed, resulting in humility, but I do not believe these are the humiliations that Father Rohr was praying for. Theologian Carol Zaleski wrote in an article on humility in the *Christian Century*, "Humiliation is an affliction; humility is a gift."[3]

INVITATION TO PRACTICE

Remember one humiliating experience that came from within and one that came from outside. How were they different, and what effect did they have on you?

We may experience the gift of humility when, through spiritual practices such as hospitality and service, our eyes are opened to a wider view of life that helps us move our attention from our individual concerns to the concerns of the world. Instead of thinking of ourselves as the center of the universe, we begin to recognize that our rightful place is in connection with others and with the whole created world. With that view, we are able to value our contribution to the interdependence of all things—at the same time, we realize we are not very important.

The poet Mark Nepo tells of climbing to the top of some cliffs in New Mexico where hundreds of Pueblo Indians had lived for twelve generations. As he and his companion looked out over the world stretching below, she said, "How beautifully insignificant we are...." Touched by his insignificance and amazed by the long history of that beautiful place, Nepo wrote later, "[Humility] gives us a connection with everything older than we are and so, provides us with a calming perspective outside of our daily worries...."[4]

INVITATION TO PRACTICE
When have you felt small, beautifully insignificant, and connected with everything older than you? What was that experience of humility like?

Cultivating Humble Hearts

Humility seems to be a gift that grows slowly from years of grateful living. Humility is a gift to be received, not achieved by our own efforts; a gift that emerges as we get out of the way; a gift that increases as it is shared with others. We can open our hearts to receive the gift of humility through a variety of spiritual practices, some of which remind us that all of life is gift, and others that help us see clearly our own gifts and limitations.

By accepting our limitations, we let go of false expectations of ourselves. We do not have to try to be perfect. We no longer need to hide our failings. Rather we are freed to be who we are and do what we are uniquely called to do. This recognition frees our special gifts to be shared with others and the world. In her poem "Famous," Naomi Shihab Nye expresses the liberation we can experience by recognizing both our gifts and our limitations:

> *I want to be famous in the way a pulley is famous,*
> *Or a buttonhole, not because it did anything spectacular,*
> *But because it never forgot what it can do.*[5]

In addition to accepting our own gifts and limitations, we must be willing to recognize and honor the gifts and limitations of others. When we welcome wholeheartedly these gifts, there is no need to be threatened by or competitive with what another has to offer. How lovely it can be to receive from others gifts that we have no talent for—such as helpful advice on the ways we might fix our broken fence, an informative explanation of a political idea that we don't understand, or a photograph of a family event when we forgot our camera.

A little more difficult is accepting the gifts of others in the area of our own abilities. When I was a teenager making my own clothes, I found it hard to see a classmate in a homemade dress that was far superior to mine. As a writer, I sometimes read a poem, essay, or story that is deeply touching, and it is not easy to simply celebrate the beauty of the words and not feel competitive with the author and wish I had written that piece myself.

INVITATION TO PRACTICE

When have you found it easy to honor the gifts of another person? When have you found it difficult?

Accepting other people's limitations is not difficult when those failings do not affect us. But when they seem to make our lives more problematic, or when those limitations cause behavior that is in opposition to our values, we will have a much harder time. I worked for an elementary school principal who was very disorganized. When he forgot to send home notices, or lost the memo from the superintendent, or interrupted my classroom with an insignificant request, my teaching became more difficult. In that same school, the teacher across the hall continually shouted at her students, trying to get and maintain control. Her lack of classroom management skills did not affect my teaching, but her limitations hurt my heart.

When we encounter such limitations in others, we are tempted to judge and to blame. Sometimes I would think that some of the issues I was having with a student were the principal's fault, when actually I had created the problem myself. When the shouting began, I was tempted to roll my eyes and feel proud of my own classroom management skills. But if we have been engaging in spiritual practice and have accepted our own limitations, we may be able to let go of judgment and blame and take a wider view. Can we pause, and breathe, and let go of being right? Can we trust that others are doing the best they can at the moment? If we decide to intervene, can we do it with a humble heart? In the paradoxical words of Brother David, "In our best moments humility is simply pride that is too grateful to look down on anyone."6

Discovering the Depth of Your Compassion

In Buddhism, compassion is defined as the wish that all beings be free of their suffering. Although we cannot rid the world of its pain, we can cultivate compassion in our own hearts, thereby helping others do the same. Compassion, which literally means to "suffer with," is not so much a feeling as a quality of being. Compassion is different from pitying another person, for although pity may come from a tender heart, it keeps us separate from the suffering of another. Pity often carries with it judgment and contempt. Sympathy and empathy, often used synonymously with compassion, are also quite different. The Greek word *pathos*, translated "feelings," is the root of these words and implies an exclusive nearness through the sharing of feelings. Whatever affects one person similarly affects the other. "I know just how you feel," are sympathetic words.

The experience of compassion is much larger, taking us beyond both the distance inherent in pity and the closeness that comes through the shared feelings of sympathy. Compassion grows when we know something of a neighbor's suffering because we can connect through similar experiences in our own life. Compassion deepens when we recognize that our neighbors, friends, and enemies alike share our humanity with us. In the words of Henri Nouwen, this partnership "cuts through all walls which might have kept you separate. Across all barriers of land and language, wealth and poverty, knowledge and ignorance, we are one, created from the same dust, subject to the same laws, and destined for the same end."[7]

INVITATION TO PRACTICE

Remember when you have experienced pity, another time sympathy, and then when you have experienced compassion. Notice the difference among the experiences.

Compassion is the fruit of practice often held up as the quality that indicates enlightenment, union with God, or spiritual maturity. If you practice faithfully, many spiritual writers proclaim, the seeds of compassion will be sown, and over time compassion will grow and flower. I have a friend who questions this wisdom. She has lived a long life of spiritual practice and has had many moments of awakening. She has touched the One, has surrendered her anger, and knows humility intimately. However, she is not experiencing the flowering of compassion. "I still judge people," she told me. "I cannot feel one with those who act unjustly, whose behavior is cruel, or who ignore the feelings of others. I guess I cannot feel compassion for those who are not compassionate." She wonders if the spiritual teachers are wrong about compassion always being a fruit of awakening or whether compassion still awaits her. She holds her question lightly as she continues to practice, knowing she may never know.

The Courage to See, the Courage to Feel, and the Courage to Act

It is not easy to enter into another person's suffering. It takes courage to become one with the oppressor as well as the oppressed, to identify with others' pain as well as joy, and to know that there is nothing in anyone else that is not in me.

At a Spiritual Directors International conference on cultivating compassion, John Philip Newell, teacher and writer from the Iona community in Scotland, organized his three talks around this theme of courage. He drew on the wisdom of Nobel Peace Laureate Aung San Suu Kyi, who believes there are three movements in the flowering of compassion—the courage to see, to feel, and to act.[8]

The courage to see is the willingness to open the eyes of our hearts and look at the suffering around us. It is tempting to turn away from the pain of others, whether that of individuals in our neighborhoods and communities or the oppression and violence suffered by millions around the world. Young children believe, when hiding their eyes, that what they were looking at no longer exists. I think we hope that if we don't see the suffering, it will not be real. We protect ourselves by hiding our eyes.

INVITATION TO PRACTICE
When you open your eyes, where do you see the
suffering of people, creatures, and the earth?

Once we have found the courage to see the pain in the world, we need more courage to feel it. Often we protect ourselves by hardening our hearts as soon as we see the pain. We acknowledge it but do not let it in. Feeling the pain of others is complex, for in doing so we may not only feel grief, we may also have to cope with anger, helplessness, judgment, and despair. But only when we feel deeply are we able to find the courage to act.

When we have seen and felt the pains of the world, our tendency is often to react, rather than respond with love and patience. In the desire for resolution we may not take the time and care to discern what action may be most appropriate to the immediate situation. Patient actions are those that emerge slowly and ultimately console, comfort, heal, and reconcile. They do not announce our personal or collective power, but rather make known the divine power that is moving the universe toward wholeness and healing.

For your compassionate heart to grow, the courage to see, feel, and act must also be directed toward your own suffering. You must include yourself in the suffering of the world. Are you willing to face your own suffering—your losses, disappointments, injuries, and illnesses? Sometimes we discount our own suffering because we see more extensive and pervasive violence and oppression around us. Comparing one suffering to another is just another way to not recognize the suffering everywhere. We all suffer in some way.

As you acknowledge your own suffering, are you able to engage and feel the pain? Our culture is quick to tell us not to feel sorry for ourselves, not to weep, and if we do, to do it in private and to do it quickly. We must honor our losses and struggles and be gentle with ourselves, trusting that the full expression of grief will eventually lead to the courage to act.

I taught with a woman whose husband died suddenly, and a week after his death she returned to school. Many people told her she should take more time, that it was not wise to return to work so soon, and that she needed time to complete her grieving. "My grief will never be complete," she replied with tears in her eyes. I need to be with the children. I can grieve and teach, teach and weep. The best thing I can do for myself is to be useful to others." Through her courage to act purposefully in the face of her suffering, this woman discovered compassion for herself.

INVITATION TO PRACTICE
When have you been compassionate with yourself?
How has it affected your compassion to others?

Just as gratefulness and humility are bound together, so are compassion and gratitude, for patient action is guided by gratitude, and gratitude gives birth to compassionate action. "The compassionate life is a grateful life," writes co-author Henri Nouwen in the book *Compassion*, "and actions born out of gratefulness are not compulsive but free, not somber but joyful, not fanatical but liberating."[9] Our compassion will not relieve all suffering, but our compassionate, humble, and grateful hearts can make a difference in some small way in the healing of the world.

The three movements of compassion could be summed up in what is known as the Golden Rule and is found in some form in many religious traditions. In Judaism and Christianity we read, "You shall love your neighbor as yourself." The Islamic version is, "Not one of you is a believer until he loves for his brother what he loves for himself." Jainism teaches, "A man should wander about treating all creatures as he himself would be treated." In Confucianism we are told to "try your best to treat others as you wish to be treated yourself." In Hinduism the rule is reversed by telling us what not to do: "One should not behave toward others in a way that is disagreeable to oneself." Similarly, from the traditional religions of Nigeria: "One going to take a pointed stick to pinch a baby bird should first try it on himself to feel how it hurts."

I used to think that this commandment to love my neighbor as myself was linear. I thought that my love for my neighbor had to come before my love of self, because that word comes first in the passage. Then I realized that the order of the words in this linear commandment was not significant. I was supposed to love myself first, which would allow me to extend that love to my neighbor. However, in the past few years, I have come to interpret this passage with nondualistic eyes. I no longer see self and neighbor as separate, one first, and the other second. I believe this rule is calling us to see and feel our neighbors *as* our selves. I am my neighbor. My neighbor is me. Or, as taught in Buddhist wisdom, "Just as I am so are they; just as they are so am I."[10] With this worldview, compassion becomes our natural response to all of creation.

How Are You Called to Practice?

Practicing the fruits of practice is more about noticing than doing. As you wake to your life as it is, pay attention to the welling up of gratitude as you experience the created world. Notice the daily surprises that fill you with thanksgiving, and watch for small blessings everywhere you turn. In the midst of struggles and the small and large difficulties of daily life, see if you can find something to be grateful for. Are you learning to be thankful *in* all things? As joy increases in your life, notice if you are grateful because of your joy or joyful because of your grateful heart. Notice if it goes both ways!

Begin to look for humble people in your life. Pay attention to those near and dear as well as people you run into at meetings, at sports events, or in the grocery store. What are the signs of humility? Then look to your own capacity for humility. When you are embarrassed or make mistakes, pay attention to whether you berate yourself or whether you are able to say to yourself, "Ah, just one more lesson in humility."

Notice how you compare yourself with others. When you acknowledge the giftedness of others, are you proud if you feel you are better than they are? Do you envy other people's gifts? Do you become competitive? When faced with other people's limitations, are you critical or dismissive, or can you look at them with compassion, knowing that you too have failings of your own?

When compassion for yourself and others arises spontaneously, pause and be grateful. When confronted with the suffering of others in news accounts, in people's stories, or in history, are you willing to see and feel the pain? Pay attention if you want to turn away and close down your heart for a moment. Sometimes it is wise to do just that. You need to be compassionate with yourself, recognizing that for your own health and well-being you might choose not to look. Allowing yourself to be overwhelmed by all that you see and feel serves no one.

Begin paying attention to how gratefulness, humility, joy, and compassion are all interacting in your life. When grateful, you may feel the movement of humility. When joyful, you may find it easier to be compassionate with yourself and others. When moved to compassion for another's pain, you may be overcome with gratefulness for some small blessing and realize you are being thankful in all things.

Noticing is the basic practice, but for those of you who wish to practice each of these fruits with more intention, I have provided three exercises to increase your awareness of gratefulness, humility, and compassion.

GUIDELINES FOR MORE EXTENDED PRACTICE

KEEPING A GRATITUDE JOURNAL

I recommend a small notebook, maybe with a pleasing cover, and I encourage you to write your gratitudes by hand rather than keeping them in a computer file. Writing by hand slows you down and allows you to linger with your memories. Plan to write in your journal at least four or five times a week.

> At the end of your first day, find a few moments to sit with your journal. Go over your waking hours, making note of the things you are grateful for.

> Do the same thing at the time of your next entry. Be sure you make note of something you are grateful for that was not included in your first list.

⇒ Continue to challenge yourself, each time you make an entry, to find something you have never written down before.

⇒ At some point you may wish to continue noticing but stop writing down the things that you list every day, such as the food you eat, and focus on newly discovered gratitudes.

⇒ As you continue this journal practice, allow yourself to be surprised by the unlikely places and ways you find blessings in your everyday life.

⇒ Some people like to enhance their journals with pictures, photographs, or small drawings.

⇒ Be aware when the journal no longer feels helpful, and ask yourself if you are now finding it easier and more natural to simply live gratefully.

DISCOVERING YOUR IMAGE OF HUMILITY

For this meditation you will need a blank piece of paper and some crayons, markers, or colored pencils.

⇒ Find a quiet place where you can be alone for thirty or forty minutes.

⇒ Settle yourself comfortably with your drawing materials near.

⇒ Close your eyes, and settle yourself with your breathing.

⇒ Bring to mind and heart people you know who are humble. Remember and imagine them as fully as possible, not analyzing them, but experiencing their presence.

⇒ As their qualities and behaviors emerge from your musings, see if you are willing to bring those qualities of humility into your own soul.

⇒ Imagine the many aspects of humility mixing and mingling within you to form an image of humility.

⇒ Don't force an image. Let it emerge slowly, noticing colors, shapes, forms, and movement. Take as long as you want.

> When you are ready, open your eyes, pick up your colors, and begin to put the image on paper. You may have difficulty capturing it exactly. Don't worry; simply allow an image to take shape on the paper before you. This is not a drawing activity so much as a way to discover what humility looks like in your experience.

> When you have completed your image, label and date it, and if possible, place it somewhere to remind you of the possibility of living with a humble heart.

KNOWLEDGE OF THE STRANGER DEEPENS COMPASSION

This is a lengthy practice that may extend over many months. It is designed from the belief that the more we know about a stranger and the more we realize what we cannot know, the more our compassion grows and deepens. In this particular exercise, the "stranger" will be a country.[11]

> Choose a country that you find attractive and intriguing. You may have visited it or not, but you have the desire to know more.

> Once or twice a month, read an article, watch a movie, or listen to the music of that country, getting to know it in a variety of ways.

> You could discover the poetry and literature of that country, study its history, experiment with its cuisine, or celebrate its national holidays.

> If the religion of this country is different from yours, it may be possible to attend a worship service. If not, find a way to familiarize yourself with their prayer forms and their traditional music.

> Seek out people from that country living within your community and initiate a conversation.

> Watch for daily news from your chosen country. What are the sufferings and celebrations of the people? Notice if your knowledge of the country gives rise to compassion,

even when what you are reading may be difficult to understand or imagine.

 Throughout these months be aware that you are breaking down barriers between yourself and others whom you once thought of as strangers. Has this affected your capacity for compassion?

ACKNOWLEDGMENTS

Writing this book has been a spiritual practice, and I have called on many of the contemplative practices to keep myself grounded and connected. Silence and solitude have been required, and I am deeply appreciative of the people and places that have provided those periods of stillness. The practices of rest and caring for my body have helped me find a rhythm within this creative process. Of utmost importance has been the ongoing practice of letting go. I had to give up favorite stories and ideas I thought were necessary. I had to let go of what I had originally thought this book would be, so it could become the book it is.

Writing and publishing a book also engage communal practices. I am thankful for the stories and lived experiences shared by my family and friends, by colleagues, students, and directees, and by the occasional stranger who appears in these pages. I am grateful for the surprising invitation issued by my editor, Emily Wichland, to write this book, and for her clear and encouraging guidance throughout the process.

I trust that writing *Fully Awake and Truly Alive* has been a missional practice as well. I write for an unknown audience with the hope that my deep gladness in some way meets the deep hunger for spiritual nurture that resides in the world today. Therefore, I am filled with gratitude for you the reader, who, in picking up this book, has received my gift. Thank you.

NOTES

1. The Practice of Caring for Your Body: Finding New Images, Deep Wisdom, and Blessings

1. Jon M. Sweeney, *Praying with Our Hands: 21 Practices of Embodied Prayer from the World's Spiritual Traditions* (Woodstock, VT: SkyLight Paths, 2000), 53.

2. Jan Phillips, *Divining the Body: Reclaim the Holiness of Your Physical Self* (Woodstock, VT: SkyLight Paths, 2005), 85.

3. Sweeney, *Praying with Our Hands*, 75.

4. Barbara Brown Taylor, *An Altar in the World: A Geography of Faith* (New York: HarperCollins, 2009), 39.

2. The Practice of Rest: Restoring Your Energy, Your Creativity, and Your Spirit

1. Thomas Merton, *Conjectures of a Guilty Bystander* (Garden City: Image Books, 1968), 86.

2. Michael Leunig, *The Curly Pyjama Letters* (Sydney: Viking Australia, 2001), 25–26.

3. To read more about Centering Prayer, see Cynthia Bourgeault, *Centering Prayer and Inner Awakening* (Cambridge, MA: Cowley Publications, 2004) or Thomas Keating, *Intimacy with God: An Introduction to Centering Prayer* (New York: Crossroad, 2009).

4. Wayne Muller, *Sabbath: Restoring the Sacred Rhythm of Rest* (New York: Bantam Books, 1999), 37.

5. Susannah Heschel, introduction to *The Sabbath*, by Abraham Joshua Heschel (New York: Farrar, Straus and Giroux, 2005), xiv.

6. Abraham Joshua Heschel, *The Sabbath* (New York: Farrar, Straus and Giroux, 1951), 101.

7. Ibid., 28–30.

3. The Practice of Silence: Finding Spaciousness, Stillness, and Inner Peace

1. Thomas Keating, *Open Mind, Open Heart: The Contemplative Dimension of the Gospel* (Amity, NY: Amity House, 1986), 53.

2. Adyashanti, *Emptiness Dancing: Selected Dharma Talks of Adyashanti* (Los Gatos, CA: Open Gate Publishing, 2004).

3. Patricia Loring, *Spiritual Discernment: The Context and Goal of Clearness Committees* (Wallingford, PA: Pendle Hill Publications, 1992), 24.

4. Jan L. Richardson, *In the Sanctuary of Women: Daily Prayers and Readings* (Nashville, TN: Upper Room Books, 2010), 35.

5. Kathleen Norris, *Amazing Grace: A Vocabulary of Faith* (New York: Riverhead Books, 1998), 17.

6. Caran Ware Joseph, unpublished paper, Iliff School of Theology, December 2011.

7. Adyashanti, *True Meditation: Discover the Freedom of Pure Awareness* (Boulder, CO: Sounds True, 2006), 21.

4. The Practice of Solitude: Making Friends with Yourself

1. Joan Chittister, *Called to Question: A Spiritual Memoir* (Lanham, MD: Sheed and Ward, 2004), 68.

2. Paul Tillich, *The Eternal Now* (New York: Charles Scribner's Sons, 1963), 17–18.

3. Henri J. M. Nouwen, *Reaching Out: The Three Movements of the Spiritual Life* (Garden City, NY: Doubleday, 1966), 22.

4. Henri J. M. Nouwen, *Clowning in Rome: Reflections on Solitude, Celibacy, Prayer, and Contemplation* (Garden City, NY: Image Books, 1979), 14.

5. Anthony Storr, *Solitude: A Return to the Self* (New York: Free Press, 1988), 17–20.

6. Thomas Merton, *A Year with Thomas Merton: Daily Meditations from His Journals*, ed. Jonathan Montaldo (New York: HarperOne, 2004), 9.

7. Phil Cousineau, *The Art of Pilgrimage: The Seeker's Guide to Making Travel Sacred* (Boston: Conari Press, 1998), xxx.

8. Eric Weiner, *Man Seeks God: My Flirtations with the Divine* (New York: Twelve Publishing, 2011), 158.

9. Kahlil Gibran, *The Prophet* (New York: Alfred A. Knopf, 1961), 16.

10. John Chryssavgis, *In the Heart of the Desert: The Spirituality of the Desert Fathers and Mothers* (Bloomington, IN: World Wisdom, 2008), 49–51.

5. The Practice of Letting Go: Releasing Your Attachments, Your Past, and Your Future

1. Phillip Harnden, *Journeys of Simplicity: Traveling Light with Thomas Merton, Bashō, Edward Abbey, Annie Dillard & Others* (Woodstock, VT: SkyLight Paths, 2003), 4.

2. Ray Buckley, quoted on http://bymyart.wordpress.com/2007/12/27/native-american-give-away-tradition/.

3. Richard Rohr, *Everything Belongs: The Gift of Contemplative Prayer* (New York: Crossroad Publishing, 2003), 27.

4. Prabhavananda and Christopher Isherwood, trans., *The Song of God: Bhagavad-Gita* (New York: New American Library, 1972), 47.

6. The Practice of Community: Discovering Support, Encouragement, and Interdependence

1. Arnie Kozak, "The Three Jewels," www.netplaces.com.

2. Lawrence A. Hoffman, *The Way Into Jewish Prayer* (Woodstock, VT: Jewish Lights Publishing, 2000), 174.

3. Cynthia Winton-Henry, *Dance—The Sacred Art: The Joy of Movement as a Spiritual Practice* (Woodstock, VT: SkyLight Paths, 2009), 151.

4. Matthew Fox, ed., *Hildegard of Bingen's Book of Divine Works: With Letters and Songs* (Santa Fe, NM: Bear and Company, 1987), 358.

5. Arthur Jones, Keynote address (11th Annual Centus Samaritan Luncheon, PPA Events Center, Denver, Colorado, May 3, 2012).

6. Spiritual Directors International, http://sdiworld.org.

7. I was introduced to this activity by Rev. Lydia Ferrante-Roseberry at an InterPlay gathering in Lafayette, Colorado, July 7, 2001.

7. The Practice of Hospitality: Inviting, Welcoming, and Nurturing the Stranger

1. "Hospitality," The Heart of Hinduism, http://hinduism.iskcon.org/lifestyle/810.htm.

2. Quoted in www.unification.net/ws/theme141.htm.

3. Orie knows I am writing this story about her. When I asked her permission she replied with the following e-mail:

    Jane, Sure! Yes!!!!!!!! Please!!!!!!!!
    I am very excited that we are in the book!
    Thank you so much.
    Could you send [the] book after [it's] published?
    We are looking forward to find[ing] our story in the book!
    Thank you, Jane!!!!!!!
    I am happy :)

4. Christine D. Pohl, *Making Room: Recovering Hospitality as a Christian Tradition* (Grand Rapids, MI: W. B. Eerdmans, 1999), 136.

5. Rumi's poem is quoted in Jack Kornfield, *After the Ecstasy, the Laundry: How the Heart Grows Wise on the Spiritual Path* (New York: Bantam Books, 2000), xi.

6. Pema Chödrön, *Comfortable with Uncertainty: 108 Teachings on Cultivating Fearlessness and Compassion* (Boston: Shambala, 2003), 77.

8. The Practice of Service: Cultivating Generosity, Kindness, and Joy

1. Eboo Patel, in *Hearing the Call across Traditions: Readings on Faith and Service*, ed. Adam Davis (Woodstock, VT: SkyLight Paths, 2009), x.

2. Quoted in Roger Walsh, *Essential Spirituality: The 7 Central Practices to Awaken Heart and Mind* (New York: Wiley, 1999), 256–57.

3. Frederick Buechner, *Wishful Thinking: A Theological ABC* (New York: HarperOne, 1993), 95.

4. Wendy Wright, "Passing Angels: The Arts of Spiritual Discernment." *Weavings: A Journal of the Christian Spiritual Life* 10, no. 6 (November/December 1985): 12.

5. Quoted in Walter Wink, *The Powers That Be: Theology for a New Millennium* (New York: Doubleday, 1998), 185.

6. Rabindranath Tagore. BrainyQuote.com, Xplore Inc, 2012. www.brainyquote.com/quotes/quotes/r/rabindrana134933.html, accessed October 28, 2012. Found on a brochure announcing the opening of a new Mind-Body Studio.

7. Stephen Mitchell, trans., *Tao Te Ching: A New English Version* (New York: HarperCollins, 1988), quoted in Wayne Muller, *Sabbath: Restoring the Sacred Rhythm of Rest* (New York: Bantam Books, 1999), 169.

9. The Fruits of Practice: Living Gratefully, Humbly, and Compassionately

1. David Steindl-Rast, *Gratefulness, the Heart of Prayer: An Approach to Life in Fullness* (Mahwah, NJ: Paulist Press, 1984), 25.

2. Ibid., 204.

3. Carol Zaleski, "The Lowly Virtue," *The Christian Century*, May 16, 2006, 33.

4. Mark Nepo, *The Book of Awakening: Having the Life You Want by Being Present to the Life You Have* (San Francisco: Conari Press, 2011), 266.

5. Naomi Shihab Nye, "Famous," *Words Under the Words: Selected Poems* (Portland, OR: Eighth Mountain Press, 1995), 80.

6. Steindl-Rast, *Gratefulness*, 203.

7. Henri J. M. Nouwen, *With Open Hands*, 2nd ed. (Notre Dame, IN: Ave Maria Press, 2006), 56.

8. John Phillip Newell, Keynote address, "Cultivating Compassion," (Spiritual Directors International Education Event, Boston, Massachusetts, April 19–26, 2012).

9. Donald P. McNeill, Douglas A. Morrison, Henri J. M. Nouwen, *Compassion: A Reflection on the Christian Life* (Garden City, NY: Doubleday, 1982), 126.

10. "The Golden Rule," World Scripture, www.unification.net/ws/theme015.htm.

11. This practice is adapted from Karen Armstrong, *Twelve Steps to a Compassionate Life* (New York: Alfred A. Knopf, 2011), 159–161.

SUGGESTIONS FOR FURTHER READING

Introduction

Aitken, Robert, and David Steindl-Rast. *The Ground We Share: Everyday Practice, Buddhist and Christian.* Boston: Shambala, 1996.

Brussat, Frederic, and Mary Ann Brussat. *Spiritual Rx: Prescriptions for Living a Meaningful Life.* New York: Hyperion, 2000.

Jones, Tony. *The Sacred Way: Spiritual Practices for Everyday Life.* Grand Rapids, MI: Zondervan, 2005.

Mackenzie, Don, Ted Falcon, and Jamal Rahman. *Getting to the Heart of Interfaith: The Eye-Opening, Hope-Filled Friendship of a Pastor, a Rabbi & an Imam.* Woodstock, VT: SkyLight Paths, 2009.

McLaren, Brian. *Finding Our Way Again: The Return of the Ancient Practices.* Nashville, TN: Thomas Nelson, 2008.

Nepo, Mark. *The Book of Awakening: Having the Life You Want by Being Present to the Life You Have.* San Francisco: Conari Press, 2011.

Walsh, Roger. *Essential Spirituality: The 7 Central Practices to Awaken Heart and Mind.* New York: Wiley, 1999.

1. The Practice of Caring for Your Body: Finding New Images, Deep Wisdom, and Blessings

Nouwen, Henri J. M. *With Open Hands.* 2nd ed. Notre Dame, IN: Ave Maria Press, 2006.

Phillips, Jan. *Divining the Body: Reclaim the Holiness of Your Physical Self.* Woodstock, VT: SkyLight Paths, 2005.

Rinpoche, Sogyal. *The Tibetan Book of Living and Dying.* Rev. ed. Edited by Patrick Gaffney and Andrew Harvey. San Francisco, CA: HarperSanFrancisco, 2002.

Sweeney, Jon M. *Praying with Our Hands: 21 Practices of Embodied Prayer from the World's Spiritual Traditions.* Woodstock, VT: SkyLight Paths, 2000.

Taylor, Barbara Brown. *An Altar in the World: A Geography of Faith*. New York: HarperCollins, 2009.

Vennard, Jane E. *Praying with Body and Soul: A Way to Intimacy with God*. Minneapolis, MN: Augsburg, 1998.

2. The Practice of Rest: Restoring Your Energy, Your Creativity, and Your Spirit

Heschel, Abraham Joshua. *The Sabbath*. New York: Farrar, Straus and Giroux, 1951.

Keating, Thomas, M. Basil Pennington, and Thomas E. Clarke. *Finding Grace at the Center: The Beginning of Centering Prayer*. 3rd ed. Woodstock, VT: SkyLight Paths, 2007.

Muller, Wayne. *Sabbath: Restoring the Sacred Rhythm of Rest*. New York: Bantam Books, 1999.

Shulevitz, Judith. *The Sabbath World: Glimpses of a Different Order of Time*. New York: Random House, 2010.

3. The Practice of Silence: Finding Spaciousness, Stillness, and Inner Peace

Cain, Susan. *Quiet: The Power of Introverts in a World That Can't Stop Talking*. New York: Crown Publishers, 2012.

Frenette, David. *The Path of Centering Prayer: Deepening Your Experience of God*. Boulder, CO: Sounds True, 2012.

Holmes, Barbara A. *Joy Unspeakable: Contemplative Practices of the Black Church*. Minneapolis: Fortress Press, 2004.

Keating, Thomas. *Open Mind, Open Heart: The Contemplative Dimension of the Gospel*. New York: Continuum, 2006.

Maitland, Sara. *A Book of Silence*. Berkeley, CA: Counterpoint, 2009.

McPherson, C. W. *Keeping Silence: Christian Practices for Entering Stillness*. Harrisburg, PA: Morehouse Publishing, 2002.

Merton, Thomas. *Dialogues with Silence: Prayers and Drawings*. Edited by Jonathan Montaldo. New York: HarperCollins Publishers, 2001.

Tolle, Eckhart. *Stillness Speaks*. Novato, CA: New World Library, 2003.

4. The Practice of Solitude: Making Friends with Yourself

Connors, Philip. *Fire Season: Field Notes from a Wilderness Lookout*. New York: Ecco, 2011.

Fisher, Lionel. *Celebrating Time Alone: Stories of Splendid Solitude*. Hillsboro, OR: Beyond Words Publishing, 2001.

Grumbach, Doris. *Fifty Days of Solitude*. Boston: Beacon Press, 1994.

Mahler, Richard. *Stillness: Daily Gifts of Solitude*. Boston: Red Wheel, 2003.

Nhat Hanh, Thich. *The Long Road Turns to Joy: A Guide to Walking Meditation.* Berkeley, CA: Parallax Press, 2011.

Paintner, Christine Valters. *Desert Fathers and Mothers: Early Christian Wisdom Sayings—Annotated and Explained.* Woodstock, VT: SkyLight Paths, 2012.

Storr, Anthony. *Solitude: A Return to the Self.* New York: Free Press, 2005.

5. The Practice of Letting Go: Releasing Your Attachments, Your Past, and Your Future

Arnold, Johann Christoph. *Why Forgive?* Maryknoll, NY: Orbis Books, 2010.

Ford, Marcia. *The Sacred Art of Forgiveness: Forgiving Ourselves and Others through God's Grace.* Woodstock, VT: SkyLight Paths, 2006.

Rohr, Richard. *Simplicity: The Freedom of Letting Go.* Rev. ed. New York: Crossroad Publishing, 2003.

Ryan, Thomas. *The Sacred Art of Fasting: Preparing to Practice.* Woodstock, VT: SkyLight Paths, 2005.

6. The Practice of Community: Discovering Support, Encouragement, and Interdependence

Guenther, Margaret. *Holy Listening: The Art of Spiritual Direction.* Cambridge, MA: Cowley Publications, 1992.

Prechtel, Daniel. *Where Two or Three Are Gathered: Spiritual Direction for Small Groups.* Harrisburg, PA: Morehouse Publishing, 2012.

Saliers, Don, and Emily Saliers. *A Song to Sing, A Life to Live: Reflections on Music as Spiritual Practice.* San Francisco: Jossey-Bass, 2005.

Winton-Henry, Cynthia. *Dance—The Sacred Art: The Joy of Movement as a Spiritual Practice.* Woodstock, VT: SkyLight Paths, 2009.

7. The Practice of Hospitality: Inviting, Welcoming, and Nurturing the Stranger

Bourgeault, Cynthia. *Centering Prayer and Inner Awakening.* Cambridge, MA: Cowley Publications, 2004.

Miller, William A. *Your Golden Shadow: Discovering and Fulfilling Your Undeveloped Self.* San Francisco: Harper & Row, 1989.

Pohl, Christine D. *Making Room: Recovering Hospitality as a Christian Tradition.* Grand Rapids, MI: W. B. Eerdmans, 1999.

8. The Practice of Service: Cultivating Generosity, Kindness, and Joy

Davis, Adam, ed. *Hearing the Call across Traditions: Readings on Faith and Service.* Woodstock, VT: SkyLight Paths, 2009.

Dougherty, Rose Mary. *Discernment: A Path to Spiritual Awakening.* Mahwah, NJ: Paulist Press, 2009.

Foster, Richard J. *Celebration of Discipline: The Path to Spiritual Growth.* 3rd ed. San Francisco: HarperSanFrancisco, 1998.

Glassman, Bernard. *Bearing Witness: A Zen Master's Lessons in Making Peace.* New York: Bell Tower, 1998.

Liebert, Elizabeth. *The Way of Discernment: Spiritual Practices for Decision Making.* Louisville, KY: Westminster John Knox Press, 2008.

Lindahl, Kay. *The Sacred Art of Listening: Forty Reflections for Cultivating a Spiritual Practice.* Woodstock, VT: SkyLight Paths, 2002.

Miller, James E. *The Art of Listening in a Healing Way.* Fort Wayne, IN: Willowgreen Publishing, 2003.

9. The Fruits of Practice: Living Gratefully, Humbly, and Compassionately

Armstrong, Karen. *Twelve Steps to a Compassionate Life.* New York: Alfred A. Knopf, 2011.

Casey, Michael. *A Guide to Living in the Truth: Saint Benedict's Teaching on Humility.* Petersham, MA: Liguori/Triumph, 2001.

The Dalai Lama. *An Open Heart: Practicing Compassion in Everyday Life.* Boston: Little, Brown, 2001.

Furey, Robert J. *So I'm Not Perfect: A Psychology of Humility.* Staten Island, NY: Alba House, 1986.

Jones, Alan and O'Neil John. *Seasons of Grace: The Life-Giving Practice of Gratitude.* Hoboken, NJ: John Wiley and Sons, 2003.

Marshall, Jay W. *Thanking and Blessing—The Sacred Art: Spiritual Vitality through Gratefulness.* Woodstock, VT: SkyLight Paths, 2007.

Nouwen, Henri J. M., Donald P. McNeill, and Douglas A. Morrison. *Compassion: A Reflection on the Christian Life.* New York: Doubleday, 1982.

Shapiro, Rami M. *The Sacred Art of Lovingkindness: Preparing to Practice.* Woodstock, VT: SkyLight Paths, 2006.

Steindl-Rast, David. *Gratefulness, the Heart of Prayer: An Approach to Life in Fullness.* New York: Paulist Press, 1984.

Worthington, Everett L. Jr. *Humility: The Quiet Virtue.* West Conshohocken, PA: Templeton Foundation Press, 2007.

INDEX OF PRACTICES

Inspiration

Finding Time for the Timeless: Spirituality in the Workweek
By John McQuiston II
Offers refreshing stories of everyday spiritual practices people use to free themselves from the work and worry mindset of our culture.
5⅛ x 6½, 208 pp, Quality PB, 978-1-59473-383-3 **$9.99**

God the *What?*: What Our Metaphors for God Reveal about Our Beliefs in God *by Carolyn Jane Bohler*
Inspires you to consider a wide range of images of God in order to refine how you imagine God. 6 x 9, 192 pp, Quality PB, 978-1-59473-251-5 **$16.99**

How Did I Get to Be 70 When I'm 35 Inside?: Spiritual Surprises of Later Life *by Linda Douty*
Encourages you to focus on the inner changes of aging to help you greet your later years as the grand adventure they can be. 6 x 9, 208 pp, Quality PB, 978-1-59473-297-3 **$16.99**

Restoring Life's Missing Pieces: The Spiritual Power of Remembering & Reuniting with People, Places, Things & Self *by Caren Goldman*
A powerful and thought-provoking look at reunions of all kinds as roads to remembering and re-membering ourselves.
6 x 9, 208 pp, Quality PB, 978-1-59473-295-9 **$16.99**

Saving Civility: 52 Ways to Tame Rude, Crude & Attitude for a Polite Planet
By Sara Hacala
Provides fifty-two practical ways you can reverse the course of incivility and make the world a more enriching, pleasant place to live.
6 x 9, 240 pp, Quality PB 978-1-59473-314-7 **$16.99**

Spiritually Healthy Divorce: Navigating Disruption with Insight & Hope
by Carolyne Call
A spiritual map to help you move through the twists and turns of divorce.
6 x 9, 224 pp, Quality PB, 978-1-59473-288-1 **$16.99**

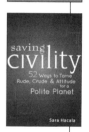

Who Is My God? 2nd Edition
An Innovative Guide to Finding Your Spiritual Identity
by the Editors at SkyLight Paths
Provides the Spiritual Identity Self-Test™ to uncover the components of your unique spirituality. 6 x 9, 160 pp, Quality PB, 978-1-59473-014-6 **$15.99**

Journeys of Simplicity
Traveling Light with Thomas Merton, Bashō, Edward Abbey, Annie Dillard & Others
by Philip Harnden
Invites you to consider a more graceful way of traveling through life. PB includes journal pages to help you get started on your own spiritual journey.
5 x 7¼, 144 pp, Quality PB, 978-1-59473-181-5 **$12.99**
5 x 7¼, 128 pp, HC, 978-1-893361-76-8 **$16.95**

Or phone, fax, mail or e-mail to: SKYLIGHT PATHS Publishing
Sunset Farm Offices, Route 4 • P.O. Box 237 • Woodstock, Vermont 05091
Tel: (802) 457-4000 • Fax: (802) 457-4004 • www.skylightpaths.com
Credit card orders: (800) 962-4544 (8:30AM–5:30PM EST Monday–Friday)
Generous discounts on quantity orders. SATISFACTION GUARANTEED. Prices subject to change.

Spirituality & Crafts

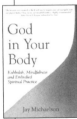

Beading—The Creative Spirit: Finding Your Sacred Center through the Art of Beadwork *by Rev. Wendy Ellsworth*
Invites you on a spiritual pilgrimage into the kaleidoscope world of glass and color. 7 x 9, 240 pp, 8-page color insert, 40+ b/w photos and 40 diagrams, Quality PB, 978-1-59473-267-6 **$18.99**

Contemplative Crochet: A Hands-On Guide for Interlocking Faith and Craft *by Cindy Crandall-Frazier; Foreword by Linda Skolnik*
Illuminates the spiritual lessons you can learn through crocheting.
7 x 9, 208 pp, b/w photos, Quality PB, 978-1-59473-238-6 **$16.99**

The Knitting Way: A Guide to Spiritual Self-Discovery
by Linda Skolnik and Janice MacDaniels Examines how you can explore and strengthen your spiritual life through knitting.
7 x 9, 240 pp, b/w photos, Quality PB, 978-1-59473-079-5 **$16.99**

The Painting Path: Embodying Spiritual Discovery through Yoga, Brush and Color *by Linda Novick; Foreword by Richard Segalman*
Explores the divine connection you can experience through art.
7 x 9, 208 pp, 8-page color insert, plus b/w photos, Quality PB, 978-1-59473-226-3 **$18.99**

The Quilting Path: A Guide to Spiritual Discovery through Fabric, Thread and Kabbalah *by Louise Silk*
Explores how to cultivate personal growth through quilt making.
7 x 9, 192 pp, b/w photos and illus., Quality PB, 978-1-59473-206-5 **$16.99**

The Scrapbooking Journey: A Hands-On Guide to Spiritual Discovery
by Cory Richardson-Lauve; Foreword by Stacy Julian Reveals how this craft can become a practice used to deepen and shape your life.
7 x 9, 176 pp, 8-page color insert, plus b/w photos, Quality PB, 978-1-59473-216-4 **$18.99**

The Soulwork of Clay: A Hands-On Approach to Spirituality
by Marjory Zoet Bankson; Photos by Peter Bankson
Takes you through the seven-step process of making clay into a pot, drawing parallels at each stage to the process of spiritual growth.
7 x 9, 192 pp, b/w photos, Quality PB, 978-1-59473-249-2 **$16.99**

Kabbalah / Enneagram
(Books from Jewish Lights Publishing, SkyLight Paths' sister imprint)

Cast in God's Image: Discover Your Personality Type Using the Enneagram and Kabbalah *by Rabbi Howard A. Addison, PhD* 7 x 9, 176 pp, Quality PB, 978-1-58023-124-4 **$16.95**

Ehyeh: A Kabbalah for Tomorrow *by Rabbi Arthur Green, PhD*
6 x 9, 224 pp, Quality PB, 978-1-58023-213-5 **$18.99**

The Enneagram and Kabbalah, 2nd Edition: Reading Your Soul
by Rabbi Howard A. Addison, PhD 6 x 9, 192 pp, Quality PB, 978-1-58023-229-6 **$16.99**

The Gift of Kabbalah: Discovering the Secrets of Heaven, Renewing Your Life on Earth *by Tamar Frankiel, PhD* 6 x 9, 256 pp, Quality PB, 978-1-58023-141-1 **$16.95**

God in Your Body: Kabbalah, Mindfulness and Embodied Spiritual Practice
by Jay Michaelson 6 x 9, 272 pp, Quality PB, 978-1-58023-304-0 **$18.99**

Jewish Mysticism and the Spiritual Life: Classical Texts, Contemporary Reflections
Edited by Dr. Lawrence Fine, Dr. Eitan Fishbane and Rabbi Or N. Rose
6 x 9, 256 pp, HC, 978-1-58023-434-4 **$24.99**

Kabbalah: A Brief Introduction for Christians
by Tamar Frankiel, PhD 5½ x 8½, 208 pp, Quality PB, 978-1-58023-303-3 **$16.99**

Zohar: Annotated & Explained *Translation & Annotation by Daniel C. Matt;*
Foreword by Andrew Harvey 5½ x 8½, 176 pp, Quality PB, 978-1-893361-51-5 **$15.99**

Spirituality

Gathering at God's Table: The Meaning of Mission in the Feast of Faith
By Katharine Jefferts Schori
A profound reminder of our role in the larger frame of God's dream for a restored and reconciled world.   6 x 9, 256 pp, HC, 978-1-59473-316-1 **$21.99**

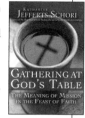

The Heartbeat of God: Finding the Sacred in the Middle of Everything
by Katharine Jefferts Schori; Foreword by Joan Chittister, OSB
Explores our connections to other people, to other nations and with the environment through the lens of faith.   6 x 9, 240 pp, HC, 978-1-59473-292-8 **$21.99**

A Dangerous Dozen: Twelve Christians Who Threatened the Status Quo but Taught Us to Live Like Jesus
by the Rev. Canon C. K. Robertson, PhD; Foreword by Archbishop Desmond Tutu
Profiles twelve visionary men and women who challenged society and showed the world a different way of living.   6 x 9, 208 pp, Quality PB, 978-1-59473-298-0 **$16.99**

Decision Making & Spiritual Discernment: The Sacred Art of Finding Your Way   *by Nancy L. Bieber*
Presents three essential aspects of Spirit-led decision making: willingness, attentiveness and responsiveness.   5½ x 8½, 208 pp, Quality PB, 978-1-59473-289-8 **$16.99**

Laugh Your Way to Grace: Reclaiming the Spiritual Power of Humor
by Rev. Susan Sparks   A powerful, humorous case for laughter as a spiritual, healing path.   6 x 9, 176 pp, Quality PB, 978-1-59473-280-5 **$16.99**

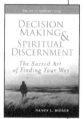

Bread, Body, Spirit: Finding the Sacred in Food
Edited and with Introductions by Alice Peck   6 x 9, 224 pp, Quality PB, 978-1-59473-242-3 **$19.99**

Claiming Earth as Common Ground: The Ecological Crisis through the Lens of Faith
by Andrea Cohen-Kiener; Foreword by Rev. Sally Bingham
6 x 9, 192 pp, Quality PB, 978-1-59473-261-4 **$16.99**

Creating a Spiritual Retirement: A Guide to the Unseen Possibilities in Our Lives
by Molly Srode   6 x 9, 208 pp, b/w photos, Quality PB, 978-1-59473-050-4 **$14.99**

Creative Aging: Rethinking Retirement and Non-Retirement in a Changing World
by Marjory Zoet Bankson   6 x 9, 160 pp, Quality PB, 978-1-59473-281-2 **$16.99**

Keeping Spiritual Balance as We Grow Older: More than 65 Creative Ways to Use Purpose, Prayer, and the Power of Spirit to Build a Meaningful Retirement
by Molly and Bernie Srode   8 x 8, 224 pp, Quality PB, 978-1-59473-042-9 **$16.99**

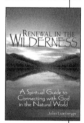

Hearing the Call across Traditions: Readings on Faith and Service
Edited by Adam Davis; Foreword by Eboo Patel
6 x 9, 352 pp, Quality PB, 978-1-59473-303-1 **$18.99**; HC, 978-1-59473-264-5 **$29.99**

Honoring Motherhood: Prayers, Ceremonies & Blessings
Edited and with Introductions by Lynn L. Caruso
5 x 7¼, 272 pp, Quality PB, 978-1-58473-384-0 **$9.99**; HC, 978-1-59473-239-3 **$19.99**

The Losses of Our Lives: The Sacred Gifts of Renewal in Everyday Loss
by Dr. Nancy Copeland-Payton   6 x 9, 192 pp, HC, 978-1-59473-271-3 **$19.99**

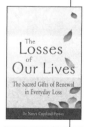

Renewal in the Wilderness: A Spiritual Guide to Connecting with God in the Natural World   *by John Lionberger*
6 x 9, 176 pp, b/w photos, Quality PB, 978-1-59473-219-5 **$16.99**

Soul Fire: Accessing Your Creativity
by Thomas Ryan, CSP   6 x 9, 160 pp, Quality PB, 978-1-59473-243-0 **$16.99**

A Spirituality for Brokenness: Discovering Your Deepest Self in Difficult Times
by Terry Taylor   6 x 9, 176 pp, Quality PB, 978-1-59473-229-4 **$16.99**

A Walk with Four Spiritual Guides: Krishna, Buddha, Jesus, and Ramakrishna
by Andrew Harvey   5½ x 8½, 192 pp, b/w photos & illus., Quality PB, 978-1-59473-138-9 **$15.99**

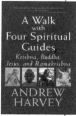

The Workplace and Spirituality: New Perspectives on Research and Practice
Edited by Dr. Joan Marques, Dr. Satinder Dhiman and Dr. Richard King
6 x 9, 256 pp, HC, 978-1-59473-260-7 **$29.99**

Women's Interest

Women, Spirituality and Transformative Leadership
Where Grace Meets Power
Edited by Kathe Schaaf, Kay Lindahl, Kathleen S. Hurty, PhD, and Reverend Guo Cheen
A dynamic conversation on the power of women's spiritual leadership and its
emerging patterns of transformation. 6 x 9, 288 pp, Hardcover, 978-1-59473-313-0 **$24.99**

Spiritually Healthy Divorce: Navigating Disruption with Insight & Hope
by Carolyne Call A spiritual map to help you move through the twists and turns of
divorce. 6 x 9, 224 pp, Quality PB, 978-1-59473-288-1 **$16.99**

New Feminist Christianity: Many Voices, Many Views
Edited by Mary E. Hunt and Diann L. Neu
Insights from ministers and theologians, activists and leaders, artists and liturgists
who are shaping the future. Taken together, their voices offer a starting point for
building new models of religious life and worship.
6 x 9, 384 pp, HC, 978-1-59473-285-0 **$24.99**

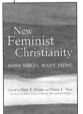

New Jewish Feminism: Probing the Past, Forging the Future
Edited by Rabbi Elyse Goldstein; Foreword by Anita Diamant
Looks at the growth and accomplishments of Jewish feminism and what they mean
for Jewish women today and tomorrow. Features the voices of women from every
area of Jewish life, addressing the important issues that concern Jewish women.
6 x 9, 480 pp, Quality PB, 978-1-58023-448-1 **$19.99**; HC, 978-1-58023-359-0 **$24.99***

Bread, Body, Spirit: Finding the Sacred in Food
Edited and with Introductions by Alice Peck 6 x 9, 224 pp, Quality PB, 978-1-59473-242-3 **$19.99**

Dance—The Sacred Art: The Joy of Movement as a Spiritual Practice
by Cynthia Winton-Henry 5½ x 8½, 224 pp, Quality PB, 978-1-59473-268-3 **$16.99**

Daughters of the Desert: Stories of Remarkable Women from Christian, Jewish
and Muslim Traditions
by Claire Rudolf Murphy, Meghan Nuttall Sayres, Mary Cronk Farrell, Sarah Conover and Betsy Wharton
5½ x 8½, 192 pp, Illus., Quality PB, 978-1-59473-106-8 **$14.99** Inc. reader's discussion guide

The Divine Feminine in Biblical Wisdom Literature
Selections Annotated & Explained
Translation & Annotation by Rabbi Rami Shapiro; Foreword by Rev. Cynthia Bourgeault, PhD
5½ x 8½, 240 pp, Quality PB, 978-1-59473-109-9 **$16.99**

Divining the Body: Reclaim the Holiness of Your Physical Self
by Jan Phillips 8 x 8, 256 pp, Quality PB, 978-1-59473-080-1 **$18.99**

Honoring Motherhood: Prayers, Ceremonies & Blessings
Edited and with Introductions by Lynn L. Caruso
5 x 7¼, 272 pp, Quality PB, 978-1-58473-384-0 **$9.99**; HC, 978-1-59473-239-3 **$19.99**

Next to Godliness: Finding the Sacred in Housekeeping
Edited by Alice Peck 6 x 9, 224 pp, Quality PB, 978-1-59473-214-0 **$19.99**

ReVisions: Seeing Torah through a Feminist Lens
by Rabbi Elyse Goldstein 5½ x 8½, 224 pp, Quality PB, 978-1-58023-117-6 **$16.95***

The Triumph of Eve & Other Subversive Bible Tales
by Matt Biers-Ariel 5½ x 8½, 192 pp, Quality PB, 978-1-59473-176-1 **$14.99**

White Fire: A Portrait of Women Spiritual Leaders in America
by Malka Drucker; Photos by Gay Block 7 x 10, 320 pp, b/w photos, HC, 978-1-893361-64-5 **$24.95**

Woman Spirit Awakening in Nature: Growing Into the Fullness of Who You Are
by Nancy Barrett Chickerneo, PhD; Foreword by Eileen Fisher
8 x 8, 224 pp, b/w illus., Quality PB, 978-1-59473-250-8 **$16.99**

Women of Color Pray: Voices of Strength, Faith, Healing, Hope and Courage
Edited and with Introductions by Christal M. Jackson
5 x 7¼, 208 pp, Quality PB, 978-1-59473-077-1 **$15.99**

The Women's Torah Commentary: New Insights from Women Rabbis on the
54 Weekly Torah Portions *Edited by Rabbi Elyse Goldstein*
6 x 9, 496 pp, Quality PB, 978-1-58023-370-5 **$19.99**; HC, 978-1-58023-076-6 **$34.95***

* A book from Jewish Lights, SkyLight Paths' sister imprint

Spiritual Practice

Fly-Fishing—The Sacred Art: Casting a Fly as a Spiritual Practice
by Rabbi Eric Eisenkramer and Rev. Michael Attas, MD; Foreword by Chris Wood, CEO, Trout Unlimited; Preface by Lori Simon, executive director, Casting for Recovery
Shares what fly-fishing can teach you about reflection, awe and wonder; the benefits of solitude; the blessing of community and the search for the Divine.
5½ x 8½, 160 pp, Quality PB, 978-1-59473-299-7 **$16.99**

Lectio Divina—**The Sacred Art:** Transforming Words & Images into Heart-Centered Prayer *by Christine Valters Paintner, PhD*
Expands the practice of sacred reading beyond scriptural texts and makes it accessible in contemporary life. 5½ x 8½, 240 pp, Quality PB, 978-1-59473-300-0 **$16.99**

Writing—The Sacred Art: Beyond the Page to Spiritual Practice
By Rami Shapiro and Aaron Shapiro
Push your writing through the trite and the boring to something fresh, something transformative. Includes over fifty unique, practical exercises.
5½ x 8½, 192 pp, Quality PB, 978-1-59473-372-7 **$16.99**

Dance—The Sacred Art: The Joy of Movement as a Spiritual Practice
by Cynthia Winton-Henry 5½ x 8½, 224 pp, Quality PB, 978-1-59473-268-3 **$16.99**

Everyday Herbs in Spiritual Life: A Guide to Many Practices
by Michael J. Caduto; Foreword by Rosemary Gladstar
7 x 9, 208 pp, 20+ b/w illus., Quality PB, 978-1-59473-174-7 **$16.99**

Giving—The Sacred Art: Creating a Lifestyle of Generosity
by Lauren Tyler Wright 5½ x 8½, 208 pp, Quality PB, 978-1-59473-224-9 **$16.99**

Haiku—The Sacred Art: A Spiritual Practice in Three Lines
by Margaret D. McGee 5½ x 8½, 192 pp, Quality PB, 978-1-59473-269-0 **$16.99**

Hospitality—The Sacred Art: Discovering the Hidden Spiritual Power of Invitation and Welcome *by Rev. Nanette Sawyer; Foreword by Rev. Dirk Ficca*
5½ x 8½, 208 pp, Quality PB, 978-1-59473-228-7 **$16.99**

Labyrinths from the Outside In: Walking to Spiritual Insight—A Beginner's Guide
by Donna Schaper and Carole Ann Camp
6 x 9, 208 pp, b/w illus. and photos, Quality PB, 978-1-893361-18-8 **$16.95**

Practicing the Sacred Art of Listening: A Guide to Enrich Your Relationships and Kindle Your Spiritual Life *by Kay Lindahl* 8 x 8, 176 pp, Quality PB, 978-1-893361-85-0 **$16.95**

Recovery—The Sacred Art: The Twelve Steps as Spiritual Practice *by Rami Shapiro;*
Foreword by Joan Borysenko, PhD 5½ x 8½, 240 pp, Quality PB, 978-1-59473-259-1 **$16.99**

Running—The Sacred Art: Preparing to Practice *by Dr. Warren A. Kay; Foreword by*
Kristin Armstrong 5½ x 8½, 160 pp, Quality PB, 978-1-59473-227-0 **$16.99**

The Sacred Art of Chant: Preparing to Practice
by Ana Hernández 5½ x 8½, 192 pp, Quality PB, 978-1-59473-036-8 **$15.99**

The Sacred Art of Fasting: Preparing to Practice
by Thomas Ryan, CSP 5½ x 8½, 192 pp, Quality PB, 978-1-59473-078-8 **$15.99**

The Sacred Art of Forgiveness: Forgiving Ourselves and Others through God's Grace
by Marcia Ford 8 x 8, 176 pp, Quality PB, 978-1-59473-175-4 **$18.99**

The Sacred Art of Listening: Forty Reflections for Cultivating a Spiritual Practice
by Kay Lindahl; Illus. by Amy Schnapper 8 x 8, 160 pp, b/w illus., Quality PB, 978-1-893361-44-7 **$16.99**

The Sacred Art of Lovingkindness: Preparing to Practice
by Rabbi Rami Shapiro; Foreword by Marcia Ford 5½ x 8½, 176 pp, Quality PB, 978-1-59473-151-8 **$16.99**

Sacred Attention: A Spiritual Practice for Finding God in the Moment
by Margaret D. McGee 6 x 9, 144 pp, Quality PB, 978-1-59473-291-1 **$16.99**

Soul Fire: Accessing Your Creativity
by Thomas Ryan, CSP 6 x 9, 160 pp, Quality PB, 978-1-59473-243-0 **$16.99**

Spiritual Adventures in the Snow: Skiing & Snowboarding as Renewal for Your Soul
by Dr. Marcia McFee and Rev. Karen Foster; Foreword by Paul Arthur
5½ x 8½, 208 pp, Quality PB, 978-1-59473-270-6 **$16.99**

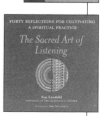

Thanking & Blessing—The Sacred Art: Spiritual Vitality through Gratefulness
by Jay Marshall, PhD; Foreword by Philip Gulley 5½ x 8½, 176 pp, Quality PB, 978-1-59473-231-7 **$16.99**

About SKYLIGHT PATHS Publishing

SkyLight Paths Publishing is creating a place where people of different spiritual traditions come together for challenge and inspiration, a place where we can help each other understand the mystery that lies at the heart of our existence.

Through spirituality, our religious beliefs are increasingly becoming a part of our lives—rather than *apart* from our lives. While many of us may be more interested than ever in spiritual growth, we may be less firmly planted in traditional religion. Yet, we do want to deepen our relationship to the sacred, to learn from our own as well as from other faith traditions, and to practice in new ways.

SkyLight Paths sees both believers and seekers as a community that increasingly transcends traditional boundaries of religion and denomination—people wanting to learn from each other, *walking together, finding the way.*

For your information and convenience, at the back of this book we have provided a list of other SkyLight Paths books you might find interesting and useful. They cover the following subjects:

Buddhism / Zen	Global Spiritual	Monasticism
Catholicism	Perspectives	Mysticism
Children's Books	Gnosticism	Poetry
Christianity	Hinduism /	Prayer
Comparative	Vedanta	Religious Etiquette
Religion	Inspiration	Retirement
Current Events	Islam / Sufism	Spiritual Biography
Earth-Based	Judaism	Spiritual Direction
Spirituality	Kabbalah	Spirituality
Enneagram	Meditation	Women's Interest
	Midrash Fiction	Worship

Or phone, fax, mail or e-mail to: SKYLIGHT PATHS Publishing
Sunset Farm Offices, Route 4 • P.O. Box 237 • Woodstock, Vermont 05091
Tel: (802) 457-4000 • Fax: (802) 457-4004 • www.skylightpaths.com
Credit card orders: (800) 962-4544 (8:30AM–5:30PM EST Monday–Friday)
Generous discounts on quantity orders. SATISFACTION GUARANTEED. Prices subject to change.